The Alpha Kappa Alpha Presence in Southwest Mississippi

*Timeless Service of
Phi Mu Omega*

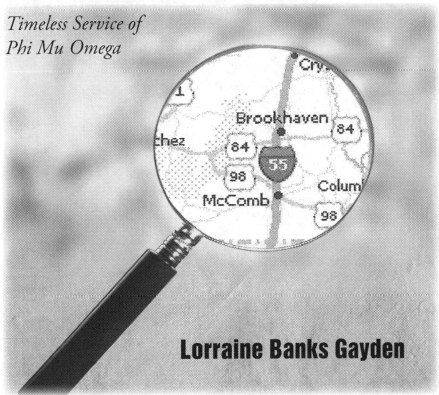

Lorraine Banks Gayden

authorHOUSE®

AuthorHouse™ LLC
1663 Liberty Drive
Bloomington, IN 47403
www.authorhouse.com
Phone: 1-800-839-8640

Published by AuthorHouse   06/27/2014

ISBN: 978-1-4918-5345-0 (sc)
ISBN: 978-1-4918-5344-3 (hc)
ISBN: 978-1-4918-5346-7 (e)

Library of Congress Control Number: 2014901525

Contents

Appendices

ABOUT THE BOOK

This book chronicles the timeless service of Phi Mu Omega chapter of Alpha Kappa Alpha from its humble beginnings as Ivy Omega Interest Group in 1998, to its chartering on January 15, 2000, to its present status as a thriving chapter living out the sorority's motto to be "Supreme in Service to All Mankind". This history book, which International President Carolyn House Stewart requested of each chapter of the Sorority, was a time-intensive and labor-intensive assignment for women who are already busy, career-minded, and community service-oriented. However, it became a labor of Love. Without her directive, this book, in all certainty, would never have been written. The project has indelibly etched a valuable lesson in the minds of the historian and chapter members—the need for archiving and documenting the chapter's programs, activities, events, and projects. The assignment has also refocused attention on previous and current international initiatives issued by each international president. According to historian Earnestine Green McNealey, Ph.D., author of the sorority's definitive history book *The Pearls of Alpha Kappa Alpha: A History of America's First Black Sorority,* "Until the lion tells its own story, the story will always glorify the hunter." This project forced chapters across the United States and in other countries to tell their own stories from their perspectives and in the context of historical events and social issues facing the communities they serve. Hopefully, it also reinforced the *raison d'etre* for every member, every chapter, every region, and the International sisterhood. This publication documents the beginning and evolving history of Phi Mu Omega for generations of young women yet to come so that they might be inspired and motivated to become women with a desire to serve all mankind.

South Eastern Region
Phi Mu Omega Chapter

History Book: Timeless Service
of Phi Mu Omega

PREFACE

Had it not been for the vision and directive of the 28th International President of Alpha Kappa Alpha Sorority, Inc., Carolyn House Stewart, Esquire, Phi Mu Omega's brief history might never have materialized and much of its history might have been lost forever. Thanks to Stewart, the story of Phi Mu Omega will now be told— from its humble beginnings as the Ivy Omega Interest Group in 1998 to its sporadic existence to its evolution as a vibrant part of the communities it serves. This project has necessarily forced current and former members to scour their closets, numerous AKA bags, boxes, and other storage places in this collaborative effort to compile the chapter's history. The previous comprehensive evaluations of the McKinzie administration had forced the chapter to dig deeply for the documentation needed. Thankfully, Phi Mu Omega successfully met the evaluation requirements without having to undergo a revisit. However, the chapter still had not secured a permanent place for its archives. It is the author's hope that the significance of this project will not be lost on current and future chapter members so that the evolving history of Phi Mu Omega will be perpetually captured for generations to come. Hopefully, young women will be inspired and motivated to become Alpha Kappa Alpha women with a desire to "be supreme in service to all mankind."

ACKNOWLEDGEMENTS

First and foremost, I would like to thank Doris Jacques, the visionary of Phi Mu Omega; Nikkita Beckley-Holloway who served as President of the Ivy Omega Interest Group; and Betty Spann Wilson-McSwain, whom 21st South Eastern Regional Director Soror Jo Celeste Pettway appointed as the first President of Phi Mu Omega.

Special thanks to Marcia Leonard for maintaining an awesome scrapbook for the chapter for the first ten years and to all the members who "stored" chapter history and documents in their homes, utility rooms, personal or commercial storage facilities; subsequent presidents, Program Chairmen, and other members who assisted with the archiving of information in the chapter's **own** storage facility secured in 2011.

I also thank the other eighteen sorors who began the journey in the Interest Group with us. Unfortunately, three of them did not become charter members of the chapter.

Thanks to Tricia Watkins, Director of Membership in Corporate Office, for providing information on former International Presidents and their program platforms.

Thanks to the former chapter presidents for the leadership skills, unique personalities, and skill sets each brought to Phi Mu Omega. Each of them left an indelible stamp on the chapter: Betty was knowledgeable and resolute; Karen had a soft but effective touch; Frances was determined and compassionate; Nikki was studious and very hands-on; Marcia brought a serious work ethic and humor; and I, being the oldest of the group, brought wisdom and gravity (see complete biographical details of chapter presidents).

I thank AKA Historian Soror Earnestine Green McNealey for her workshops and guidance in doing historical writing. After all, she wrote the definitive history of the Sorority (*The Pearls of Alpha Kappa*

Alpha: A History of America's First Black Sorority). I also thank our Corporate and Regional staff for supplying guidelines and timetables for this project.

I offer special thanks to my tech-savvy members Claudia Moore and Ruby Husband, other members of the Archives Committee—Doris Jacques, Barbara Scott, Marcia Leonard, Frances Hogan, Madeleine Floyd, Mary Helena Thompson, and Karen Luckett—who helped me put the finishing touches on the book, and every member who supplied personal information, sent emails, made phone calls, etc. I personally thank Soror Mary E. Scott of Greenville, MS, for her voluntary and professional editorial assistance. Scott is a genuine "pearl"! I especially thank Phi Mu Omega for providing the financial support and resources needed to make this project become a reality. It is my sincere hope that the chapter is pleased with and proud of the final product.

Lorraine Banks Gayden,
Author and Editor
October 2013

CHAPTER I

INTRODUCTION
(THE NINETIES)

During the 1990's, the United States was enjoying a period of relative well-being. There was general economic prosperity. George H. W. Bush was President, the unemployment rate was 5.3%, the median household income was $29,943, gas was $1.16 a gallon, and a postage stamp was $.25. With the election of William Jefferson "Bill" Clinton in 1992, the economic landscape looked even better. Although his administration was not without its controversy because of his impeachment hearings related to the Monica Lewinsky sex scandal, by the end of his two terms in 2000, the United States experienced its largest budget surplus since 1951. The unemployment rate was down to 4.9%, the median income was up to $38,568, the cost of a gallon of gas had dropped to $1.06, and a postage stamp cost $.32. Overall, most US citizens were feeling relatively calm and secure.

Meanwhile, events in the '90's global community were diverse, tumultuous, and far reaching. The prevailing world view was characterized by freedom: Nelson Mandela was freed after serving 27 years in prison in South Africa, and Lech Walesa was elected the first President of Poland after a surge against Communism. The LBGT (Lesbian, Bisexual, Gay, and Transgendered) community was "uncloseted" or freed, although not generally accepted until the Netherlands became the first county to legalize the deviant sexual behaviors in 2001.

The collapse of the Soviet Union (the USSR) and the repeal of the apartheid laws in South Africa in 1991(reminiscent of the Jim Crow laws of the South in the 1950's and '60's), and the official end of the cold war in 1992 contrasted with the 1991 onset of Operation Desert Storm, the US attack on Iraq for its invasion of Kuwait in the Middle East. The Los Angeles riots also occurred in 1992 after policemen

1

who were captured on video brutally beating Rodney King received a non-guilty verdict. The internet explosion and the World Trade Center bombings occurred in 1993 and, let's not forget, this was also the year that Lorena Bobbitt took brutal revenge on her husband for his alleged infidelity.

Ironically, just four years after his release from his 27-year imprisonment and three years after the abolishment of the apartheid system, Nelson Mandela was elected President of South Africa in 1994. Meanwhile, on another part of the African continent, the Rwandan genocide was occurring when the Hutus nearly annihilated the Tutsis. In her novel *Left to Tell*, Immaculee Ilibagiza chronicles the genocide in chilling details. Southwest Mississippi was privileged to host the author at the Southwest Mississippi Community College Fine Arts Auditorium on January 18, 2009, to hear her relate incidents first-hand, respond to questions from the audience, and autograph copies of the book. American-born terrorists made headlines on April 19, 1995, when Terry McVeigh and Terry Nichols bombed the Arthur Murray Federal Building in Oklahoma City, Oklahoma. In the Middle East, assassins killed Israeli Prime Minister Yitzhak Rabin. When Tiger Woods won the Master's Tournament in 1997, a great sense of pride filled the African—and Asian-American citizens in the United States.

In 1998, when Phi Mu Omega was in its formative stage, both troubling and remarkable events occurred. On January 29, a bomb exploded at a Birmingham, Alabama, abortion clinic, killing one and wounding several others. In February, the United States Congress authorized President Clinton to take actions against the threats of Iraq's weapons of mass destruction program in what became known as Operation Desert Fox, and Sadaam Hussein agreed with United Nations Secretary Kofi Annan to allow weapons inspectors to return to Baghdad to prevent military action by the United States and its British ally. On March 5, United States Air Force Lieutenant Colonel Eileen Collins became the first woman to command a future Space Shuttle Columbia mission. Sadly, on February 1, 2003, the Space Shuttle Columbia disintegrated over Texas during reentry, killing all seven astronauts.

The cloning of "Dolly" the sheep and the founding of Google in Menlo Park, California, by two Stanford University Ph. D. candidates were remarkable events that occurred during the 1990's. India and Pakistan conducted nuclear tests that caused the United States and Japan to impose economic sanctions on India because India conducted additional nuclear tests. In August 1998, attacks on US embassies in Dar es Salaam, Tanzania, and Nairobi killed 224 and injured over 4500. Most attacks were linked to Osama bin Laden, an exile of Saudi Arabia and the alleged head of Al Qaeda. The United States military quickly retaliated by launching cruise missiles against Al Qaeda in Afghanistan and a chemical plant in Sudan. Eventually, President Clinton and Great Britain ordered airstrikes on Iraq and weapons inspectors withdrew.

Meanwhile, back in the United States, white supremacists murdered African-American James Byrd in Jasper, Texas, for no apparent reason other than that he was black, vulnerable, and accessible. Closer to home in Mississippi, a court convicted 17-year old Pearl High School student Luke Woodham for the October 1, 1997, rampage which killed two students and wounded seven others. Woodham had allegedly stabbed and bludgeoned his mother earlier that morning before driving her car to school and shooting the others. The Columbine, Colorado, High School killing spree occurred in 1999. Contrasted with these externally violent events was the subtle sexual molestation of boys by Catholic priests. In July of 1998, the Dallas, Texas, diocese had agreed to pay $23.4 million to nine (9) alleged victims.

It was during this milieu that Doris Jacques conceived a plan for a graduate chapter of Alpha Kappa Alpha Sorority, Inc. in Southwest Mississippi.

Introduction to Southwest Mississippi

Phi Mu Omega, with its beginnings in McComb and Brookhaven, Mississippi, is located in the Southwest Mississippi area. Southwest Mississippi consists of ten counties (Adams, Amite, Claiborne, Franklin, Jefferson, Lawrence, Lincoln, Pike, Walthall, and Wilkinson). The western edge borders the nation's longest river, the mighty Mississippi River ("Father of Waters"), so named by Native American tribes indigenous to the area. The eastern border consists of Lawrence and Walthall counties. The central and northern counties are Amite, Pike, Franklin, and Lincoln. McComb (in Pike County) and Brookhaven (in Lincoln County) became the nucleus of the chapter's domicile and service activities.

Southwest Mississippi is racially and economically diverse. The river counties are renowned for their historic areas and bustling industries as a result of the gaming venues and marine transportation. Adams County still has many pre-civil war homes and plantations that are the sight of annual pilgrimages and festivals. Its major city Natchez is home to a thriving casino-and tourist-dominated economy. Zeta Delta Omega chapter in Natchez is much older than Phi Mu Omega. Claiborne County has several claims to fame as the home of one of Mississippi's HBCU's, Alcorn State University, one of the oldest land grant universities in the United States; the "Ruins of Windsor Castle," used and then burned by Union troops during the Civil War; the famous church in Port Gibson with the metal hand as the steeple pointing skyward which Union troops deemed "too beautiful to burn"; and the state's only nuclear plant Grand Gulf. Jefferson county, between Claiborne and Adams counties, elected the first well known African-American mayor in the State—Charles Evers of Fayette, brother of the late Medgar Wiley Evers, an icon of the Civil Rights Movement. Under Charles Evers' leadership, the county secured a large federal grant to build a comprehensive health care center which provided accessible and preventive medical treatment for its residents.

Wilkinson County is also home to several antebellum homes and several towns with names reminiscent of military operations during the civil war (Ft. Adams, Ft. Rosalie, etc.). There is little industry in the county except for timber farming, although it was once the location of the Carter Manufacturing Company, maker of children's clothing sold nationwide. Ironically, Phi Mu Omega member Madeleine Floyd and her husband Charlie leased the facility for recreational, fitness and athletic training purposes for several years after its closure. Amite and Franklin counties' economic bases are primarily timber production and harvesting. Gloster (in Amite county) was once home to a large wood-processing plant (Georgia Pacific) which opened in 1965 and closed in 1999. Dairy farming is also prevalent in Amite County. Franklin County is home to the Homochitto National Forest, named for an early Indian tribe in the area.

On the southeastern edge of the region is Walthall County, known as the "cream pitcher" of Mississippi, with its county seat of Tylertown. The county once had a branch of the Carter Company and other small factories but now has little or no industry or manufacturing. Some Alpha Kappa Alpha members from Walthall County are members of Mu Xi Omega chapter in Columbia, MS, in neighboring Marion County, and several are members of Phi Mu Omega chapter. Lawrence County forms the northeastern border of Southwest Mississippi. Monticello in Lawrence County has several wood-processing Georgia Pacific operations. The county previously had other manufacturing plants that have closed.

Located in the center of Southwest Mississippi are Pike and Lincoln counties. Pike County has one midsized municipality McComb (population approximately 13,644 based on the 2010 census), several smaller towns (Summit, the county seat of Magnolia, and Osyka), and several unincorporated communities. A once-thriving Catholic boarding school, St. Mary of the Pines, in Chatawa, now serves as a retirement home for the School Sisters of Notre Dame. The centerpieces of the region are McComb, "The Camellia City of America," in Pike county and Brookhaven, "Homeseekers' Paradise," in Lincoln county.

McComb and Brookhaven

McComb, named for railroad baron Colonel Henry Simpson McComb, is the retail center for much of Southwest Mississippi and got its start as a railroad town because its founder was seeking a place of refuge for his employees—presumably because of the vices and bawdiness of New Orleans. He decided to settle about 100 miles north of New Orleans. Southwest Mississippi Regional Medical Center, the Cardiovascular Institute of Mississippi, and the Mississippi Cancer Institute—all major employers—are located in McComb. In addition, Sanderson Farms poultry processing plant and Croft Metals are large employers in Pike County. The town of Summit, which reportedly earned its name because it is the highest point between New Orleans and Memphis, is home to Southwest Mississippi Community College. McComb is home to pop music icon and actress Brandy and her brother Ray J, actress Aunjanue Ellis, the late bluesman Bo Didley, Vashti Jackson and a few lesser known entertainers. Britney Spears attended Parklane Academy in McComb.

About twenty miles due north of McComb is Brookhaven, also a midsized city of approximately 12,520 people based on the 2010 census. A few small unincorporated towns are located in Lincoln County, but Brookhaven has attracted several major industries during the past 25-30 years, including the General Motors Delphi Packard plant, the Wal-Mart Distribution Center and commercial fleet, and the now—closed Jacobson Manufacturing Plant, producer of lawn mowers and equipment. Brookhaven is the home of King's Daughters Medical Center, a regional medical facility, and other industries. The Mississippi School for the Arts is on the original campus of Whitworth College, formerly a women's college, in downtown Brookhaven, and Lincoln County is part-proprietor of Copiah-Lincoln Community College in Wesson. Brookhaven has one of only two movie theaters in Southwest Miss—Natchez has the other one.

To the north of Southwest Mississippi is Copiah County (Hazlehurst) which abuts Hinds County, home of the state capitol in Jackson and HBCU Jackson State University. Jackson is also the domicile of two large graduate chapters of Alpha Kappa Alpha—Beta Delta Omega and Rho Lambda Omega. Copiah County itself is home to Copiah-Lincoln Community College, the chief industry of the county. Southwest Mississippi seemed to be the perfect place for a graduate chapter of Alpha Kappa Alpha Sorority, Inc.

CHAPTER II

THE BEGINNINGS OF PHI MU OMEGA CHAPTER

The Visionary of Phi Mu Omega

Doris Jacques

The visionary of Phi Mu Omega is Doris Washington Jacques. Four young Alpha Kappa Alpha women (biological sisters Lorraine Banks Gayden and Bobbie Banks Jackson of Gamma Rho chapter (Jackson State) and Sonja Bates Norwood (Brandy's mom) and Beverly Bates Nobles of Beta Psi chapter (Southern University in Baton Rouge, LA) discussed forming a graduate chapter in the early 1970's, but not enough sorors could be identified in McComb at the time. Jacques, who became a member of Gamma Kappa chapter at Tuskegee Institute in Tuskegee, Alabama, in 1957 and lived outside the United States in the 1970's, was not known to these younger sorors. Gayden, the oldest of the four, was only 10 years old when Jacques was initiated!

Doris Washington Jacques was born in Summit, Mississippi, in Pike County on June 10, 1936, the second of three children born to Joe Louis and Gladys Jennings Washington. Doris attended Walnut St. Elementary School, a school constructed for black children in Summit, MS, from 1941 to 1950. She then attended the all-black Burglund High School in McComb, where Professor Commodore Dewey (C.D.) Higgins was the principal, and graduated in 1954. Doris enrolled at Tuskegee and graduated in May of 1959 with a B.S. degree in secondary education. While at Tuskegee, she met and married Jamaican architect Alfonso Jacques and flew off to Kingston, Jamaica, in January 1960, where three of her four children were born. Her oldest son Tony was born in Tuskegee.

In Kingston, Doris was a substitute teacher at Mona Prep for a short period. She also worked as an administrative officer in the Jamaican government at the Ministry of Agriculture from June 1960 to September 1963 and at the Ministry of Local Government from 1967-68. In the interim, she and her family, which now included two daughters (both presently sorority members) and two sons, spent two school years on the campus of the University of British Columbia in Vancouver, Canada, where her husband received a Master's in Town and Country Planning. The family returned to Jamaica in 1965. Doris spent most of her time in Jamaica on an estate in the hills above Kingston. She returned to Summit briefly in 1968 and taught for one school term at Eva Gordon Elementary School (now South Pike) in Magnolia. Interestingly, Eva Gordon was named for former chapter member Celia Gordon Pearson's grandmother. Doris then returned to Tuskegee where she worked for one year at Debra Wolf High School and one year at the Tuskegee Federal Credit Union while her husband worked for "Model Cities." Then it was back to Jamaica in 1971. She returned to the United States in 1977, where she built a home on the family property where she was born. She worked for the Southwest Mississippi Mental Health Complex as Coordinator of Records for the ten counties in Southwest Mississippi until her retirement in December 1998. Doris says, "The experience at SMMHC was God-sent. The people that I worked with, that I met and what God took me to and what God brought me through have been a blessing in my life." She has five grandchildren who never cease to amaze her. She considers her more than 55 years of

Alpha Kappa Alpha membership a blessing, and she is truly the epitome of an Alpha Kappa Alpha woman.

Ivy Omega Interest Group

In 1998, Doris began contacting Alpha Kappa Alpha women in Pike County about organizing a graduate chapter in Southwest MS. Zeta Delta Omega chapter in Natchez was at least 70 miles away; Theta Sigma Omega in Hattiesburg was about the same distance from McComb, and Xi Mu Omega in Columbia was about 45 miles away. At the first meeting on July 19, 1998, only Doris and Marcia Scott Leonard, a 1986 Mississippi Valley State University initiate into Epsilon Pi chapter, were present. The next meeting was on October 18, 1998, with ten inactive members in attendance. All present agreed that there was a need for a chapter in their immediate service area. The members agreed to establish an interest group. Subsequent meetings were in November and December of that year.

Eventually, nineteen inactive members received clearance from the Corporate Office on February 23, 1999, and the Ivy Omega Interest Group was getting closer to its goal. Originally, Ivy Omega consisted of members living in Pike, Lincoln, Amite, and Lawrence counties. Officers of Ivy Omega were Nikkitta Beckley-Holloway, President; Doris Jacques, Vice President; Lillie M. Turner, secretary; Julia Wright Parker, assistant secretary; Marcia Leonard, financial secretary; Betty Spann Wilson, treasurer; LaTarchia Catchings Jackson, corresponding secretary; Zelphia Taylor, hostess; Nancy Denham, doorkeeper; Karen Bryant Luckett, DMD, *Ivy Leaf* Reporter; Lorraine B. Gayden, historian; and Cynthia Bryant, chaplain. On April 24, 1999, members from established chapters conducted workshops for the group. Pat Magee of Rho Lambda Omega in Jackson covered parliamentary procedures; Shirley Mays and Kimberly Dowe of Upsilon Upsilon Omega in Canton discussed chapter operations and sisterly relations respectively; and Zelmarine Murphy of Mu Xi Omega in Vicksburg discussed protocol on May 8, 1999. All were very helpful because some group members had been inactive for as many as 30 years or more! Following the orientation sessions required by corporate and regional office,

Regional Director Pettway met with the Interest Group members in Brookhaven at the Brookhaven Bank State Room on June 5, 1999, to provide further instructions for becoming a chapter and reviewed the Ivy Omega Interest Group package. Betty Wilson attended the Leadership Seminar in Orlando, FL, in July. In September Ivy Omega submitted its chartering package to Pettway, listing 16 potential charter members. On September 29, 1999, Pettway recommended to International President Norma Solomon White and the Board of Directors that Ivy Omega become the newest chapter in the South Eastern region. On November 8, 1999, Ivy Omega members received the long-awaited news: the Board of Directors (Directorate) had approved the request to charter the new chapter in Southwest Mississippi!

As Ivy Omega Interest Group, supreme service was our goal. The group eagerly embraced International President White's ON TRACK programs, and the group had completed several projects prior to its official designation in November 1999. On April 26th, the group provided snacks at the Boys and Girls Club in Brookhaven in recognition of academic and social excellence, for Linda Talbert and Valerie Jones' Girl Scout troop #142 in McComb for excelling in cookie sales, and for a troop led by Salena Washington in McComb for a great academic year. The group had fielded a team in April for the American Cancer Society's Relay for Life in McComb to address the health initiative. On May 5th, the group partnered with the Department of Human Services on "Welfare to Workfare" classes in Hazlehurst and McComb for the economic empowerment initiative. On May 14th, the group purchased and donated trophies for the Awards Day ceremony for member Cynthia Bryant's art class in New Hebron to support the arts. In May, the group donated encyclopedias, dictionaries, books, and school supplies for the shoe box project under the education target. For leadership development that year, the group held its first retreat on August 26th. On September 2nd, the group held "Family Day in the Park" to address the black family target. On September 17th the group participated in the shoe box collection project for African children. The group also donated school supplies to Alexander Junior High School, where member Zelphia Taylor taught. Other service programs during this time included AKA Coat Day in

October, Buckle Up Month in November when members distributed flyers and stickers, and the signature "Holiday" blood drive in December. On New Year's Eve 1999, the group held its first annual Scholarship Ball with a live band at the Brookhaven-Lincoln County Multipurpose Building amid all the Y2K speculations. To our delight everything went according to schedule, nothing unusual happened, and all had a good time. To the group's extreme delight, Pettway set the chartering date for January 15, 2000—the month and date of Alpha Kappa Alpha's birth!

CHAPTER III

THE CHARTERING PROCESS

Charter Members (Profiles)

Nikkitta Beckley-Holloway

Nikki was a Hazlehurst, MS (Copiah county) native, who now resided in Brookhaven after being initiated into Theta Sigma Omega in Hattiesburg, about 70 miles east of McComb. Holloway had earned degrees in Accounting from the University of Southern MS (Hattiesburg) and Mississippi College (Clinton). She was the business manager of the Hazlehurst School District. Nikki married Dexter Holloway, a member of Alpha Phi Alpha Fraternity. Nikki would later become a president of Phi Mu Omega (See chapter VI for complete bio).

Cynthia Bryant

Cynthia's parents, Mr. and Mrs. C. C. Bryant, Jr., were originally from McComb, but Cynthia grew up in Monticello in Lawrence County. She lived and worked as a teacher in the Lawrence County School District. A granddaughter of the civil rights icon and patriarch C.C. Bryant of McComb, Cynthia became a member of Gamma Phi chapter at Alcorn State in 1992. Her tenure with the chapter was short due to a career change.

LaTarcha Jackson Catchings

LaTarcha became a member of Gamma Rho chapter at Jackson State University. She lived in the service area at the time. Her tenure with the chapter was short-lived due to a move from Southwest MS.

Nancy Winston Denham

Nancy grew up in Chicago but returned to MS to attend Alcorn State University, where she became a member of Gamma Phi chapter in 1956. Nancy had retired in 1995 after being an elementary school teacher in Port Gibson and Hazlehurst for more than 30 years. She had resided in Brookhaven for some time. She had earned a Master's degree from Mississippi College. She became a "Golden" Girl in 2006 at the South Eastern Regional Conference in Memphis, TN. (See Golden Girls in appendix for biography).

Lorraine Banks Gayden

A native of McComb, Lorraine became a member of Gamma Rho chapter at Jackson State on November 19, 1966. Gayden had earned a Bachelor of Arts degree in English at Jackson State, a Master of Arts degree in English from Purdue University in W. Lafayette, IN, and an Education Specialist degree in secondary education from the University of Southern MS. In 1981, she had become the 3rd African-American county welfare director in the state of MS. In 2000, she was an English teacher at McComb High School. She would later become a president of Phi Mu Omega and a life member of the Sorority. (See chapter VI for complete bio).

Frances Bennett Hogan

A native and lifelong resident of McComb, Frances was one of fourteen (14) children. She had earned a Bachelor's degree in Business from Alcorn State University, where she became a member of Gamma Phi chapter in 1971. She had worked in the accounting department of a large manufacturing company in Magnolia, MS, but she entered the teaching profession in the McComb School District in 2001. Frances would later become the first chapter president to serve two consecutive terms from 2006-2009. (See chapter VI for complete bio).

Doris Washington Jacques

A native of Summit, Doris received her Bachelor's degree from Tuskegee Institute in Tuskegee, Alabama. She was the visionary organizer of Phi Mu Omega who became a member of Gamma Kappa chapter in 1957. Doris worked as Coordinator of Records for the Southwest Mississippi Mental Health Agency, where she began the interest group meetings at her office on South Broadway in McComb on Sunday afternoons. She would become a "Golden" Girl in 2007 at the South Eastern Regional Conference in Nashville, TN. (See chapter II for complete biography).

Marcia Scott Leonard

A native of McComb, Marcia enrolled at Mississippi Valley State University where she became a member of Epsilon Pi chapter in 1986. She later transferred to Grambling State University in Grambling, LA, where she received her Bachelor's degree in Accounting in 1988. At the time of chartering, Leonard was the financial officer for a community action agency headquartered in Lawrence County. She would later serve as chapter president (See chapter VI for complete bio).

Karen Bryant Luckett, DMD

Karen is a native of McComb. She became a member of Gamma Omicron chapter at Tougaloo College in 1986. Karen earned a B.S. degree in biology in 1987 and then enrolled at the University Of Mississippi School Of Dentistry in Jackson, where she obtained her DMD in 1991. At the time of chartering, she had moved back to McComb from Jackson and opened her private practice of general dentistry. She would become the second President of Phi Mu Omega (See chapter VI for complete bio).

Julia Wright Parker

A native of Brookhaven and a Jackson State grad, Julia became a member of Gamma Rho chapter in 1989. Julia earned a B.A. degree in Political Science at JSU and a Master's in Public Administration from the University of MS (Ole Miss). She was a caseworker with the MS. Dept. of Public Welfare in Hazlehurst and McComb for years before accepting a job at Copiah-Lincoln Community College.

Zelphia Robinson Taylor

Zelphia is a McCombite who became a member of Gamma Phi chapter at Alcorn in 1993. (Zelphia, Cynthia, and Karen are cousins.) Although she continued to live in McComb, Zelphia worked in the Brookhaven School system as a math teacher at the time. After several years, Taylor left the chapter to attend to her increasing family size and obligations. Unfortunately, Zelphia suffered a debilitating stroke in 2010 which left her unable to work.

Margaret (Wilson) Therrell
A resident of Brookhaven, Margaret was a long-time chemistry and science teacher in the Brookhaven public schools after graduating from Alcorn State University, where she became a member of Gamma Phi in 1957. Therrell was retired when the chapter was chartered, but she and her husband continue to operate several businesses in Brookhaven. She became one of the chapter's "Golden" Girls in 2007 at the South Eastern Regional Conference in Nashville, TN (See Golden Girls in appendix for biography).

Mary Helena (Ross) Thompson
A native of Lawrence County who has resided in her husband's native county (Amite) for more than 40 years, Mary Helena graduated from Alcorn State, where she became a member of Gamma Phi chapter in 1965. She was a public school teacher in the Franklin County School System for more than thirty years until her retirement in 2002. Her daughter Lakeisha Thompson Morton became a member of Gamma Phi in 1998.

Esther Kennedy Tillman
A resident of Brookhaven, Esther graduated from Jackson State. While attending graduate school at the University of Southern MS, Tillman became a member of Theta Sigma Omega in Hattiesburg. She taught in the Brookhaven schools. Her two daughters Joyce and Elizabeth would become legacy members of Phi Mu Omega in 2003 and 2007 respectively. In 2008, Tillman moved to Jackson.

Lillie M. Turner
A native of Lincoln County, Lillie became a member of Xi Mu Omega chapter in Columbia, MS, in 1980. Lillie had degrees in counseling and had served as a counselor in the McComb, Brookhaven, and Hazlehurst school districts. Lillie served as secretary of Ivy Omega Interest Group and remained a member of Phi Mu Omega until her untimely death in March 2001. Chapter members conducted the appropriate ceremony during visitation at Williams Mortuary in Brookhaven. Members also attended and participated in the homegoing service at Center Street Church of Christ in Brookhaven. Subsequently, the chapter initiated the Lillie M. Turner Memorial Scholarship

which continues to be awarded annually (see chapter on Significant Membership Changes).

Betty Spann Wilson
A native of Jackson and a resident of Brookhaven, Betty was a co-initiate into Gamma Omicron chapter at Tougaloo with Luckett in 1986. Betty had earned a Bachelor's degree in Physics from Tougaloo and a Master's degree in Educational Leadership from Delta State University (Cleveland, MS), and an Educational Specialist's Degree from Mississippi College. After teaching stints in Clarksdale, MS, Helena and W. Helena, Arkansas, Betty had moved to Southwest Mississippi to serve as an Assistant Principal at McComb High School and had met and married a basketball coach from Brookhaven.

The Chartering

The chartering ceremony and reception for Phi Mu Omega took place on January 15, 2000, at Southwest Mississippi Regional Medical Center. During the actual chartering ceremony, Soror Pettway appointed Betty Spann Wilson as President and Lorraine B. Gayden as Secretary. Members elected other officers. The reception followed in the Craig Haskins Community Room of the Medical Center. Fortuitously, Phi Mu Omega shares the same birth date as the sorority, albeit it 92 years later. Hostesses for the reception were members of Xi Mu Omega of Columbia, MS, and Upsilon Upsilon Omega of Canton, MS. Barbara Hilliard of Beta Delta Omega also attended. Chef's Delight of McComb catered the reception, EB & Co. provided entertainment, and Alford's Flowers of McComb and Toot's Florist of Brookhaven handled corsages and floral arrangements. Soror Celia Gordon Pearson, who returned to McComb from California, attended the reception and immediately decided to join Phi Mu Omega. She missed being a charter member by a few months. Ironically, her aunt and sorority member Dr. Dorothy Gordon Gray—a native of Pike County, a renowned professor at Alcorn State University, and a longtime member of Beta Delta Omega in Jackson, MS—was five days older than Alpha Kappa Alpha Sorority!! "Dot Tee", as Celia affectionately called her, was born January 10, 1908.

Charter Officers

Regional Director Pettway appointed the President and Secretary. Phi Mu Omega Charter Officers who would serve for two years were:

President ------------------- Betty Spann Wilson (now McSwain)
Vice President ------------ Karen Bryant Luckett
Secretary ------------------ Lorraine B. Gayden
Assistant Secretary ------ Julia W. Parker
Financial Secretary ------ Mary Helena Ross Thompson
Corr. Secretary ----------- Zelphia Taylor
Treasurer ------------------ Nikkitta Beckley-Holloway
Hostess -------------------- Frances B. Hogan
Chaplain------------------- Margaret W. Therrell
Parliamentarian ---------- Lillie W. Turner
Historian ------------------ Doris Jacques
Doorkeeper --------------- Nancy Denham

Celia Pearson was installed as Treasurer and Marcia Leonard was installed as *Ivy Leaf* Reporter on January 21, 2001. Monesa Watts reactivated in January 2001 and was named Parliamentarian following the untimely death of Turner on March 26, 2001. Yolanda Young also reactivated in February of 2001.

Charter Member Reflections

As newly reactivated members of the sorority, interest group members wrote memorable personal statements detailing their reason(s) for wanting to reactivate and establish a graduate chapter. Most remembered their days on college campuses, the camaraderie, the social status and prestige, and other benefits that prompted them to become members of Alpha Kappa Alpha.

A review of those statements revealed anticipation, great expectations, lots of promise for community activities and service, a desire for sisterhood, a commitment to upholding the high principles of the beloved Sorority, a desire to renew the enthusiasm in sisters who remained inactive, and a commitment to serve in their respective communities as role models and mentors for girls. In 1999, Visionary and Charter Historian Doris wrote, "We seem to have lost faith and hope, but as strong Alpha Kappa Alpha women (sic) we will encourage the community and particularly the black community to be revived, renewed, reassured, and empowered for courageous living . . . ." In 2013, she wrote "As we approach our 14th year of service as a chapter, let us reflect on our great achievement. We have had a glorious past and we are planning a wonderful, successful future. I am confident that we will reach, teach, touch and love many more young people with scholarships, reading programs, lifting of young women through EYL, cotillions, sending seeds and money to Africa, our cancer drive, and local leadership seminars. All was accomplished through awesome sisterhood and spirited service. We continue to grow in spirit and roll in spirit. We have grown and matured beyond our wildest dream. Our attitudes transcend deceit, deception, and divisiveness; yet through it all, we have progressed and become better for it. We are elegant and sophisticated, and we present charm and grace. We are fabulous divas and I am proud to call you Sorors." In 1999, her words were prophetic. In 2014, they ring true for Phi Mu Omega.

Charter President Betty wrote in 1999, "A positive Alpha Kappa Alpha impact in this locality would inspire young ladies to mimic our efforts and seek membership in this great Sorority . . ."

Betty's words have come to fruition as we have seen many of our protégés and scholarship winners go on to join our great sisterhood. In 2013 Betty reflected ". . . Alpha Kappa Alpha women have traditionally responded in times of crisis and birthed new initiatives to address social and economic trends. Phi Mu Omega members continue to bring concerted efforts to address health, education, the family and economic empowerment. I am proud that we have provided numerous scholarships, financial support, and information to enhance the quality of life for Southwest Mississippians. The call to serve has also provided the opportunity to network and bring social events that solidify the Alpha Kappa Alpha presence in our communities." In addition, she continued, "Our chapter has grown as chapter leaders take pride in being aware and supportive of the international platform(s) of our sisterhood. As Charter President, it is rewarding to continue to grow under the leadership of those who have served subsequently. Phi Mu Omega continues to chart an onward and upward course. As members of Alpha Kappa Alpha Sorority, Inc., we humbly subscribe to serving all mankind; and *by merit and culture we strive and we do.*"

Charter Vice President Karen wrote in 1999 that . . . . "Alpha Kappa Alpha women already play integral roles in our community in that many of them are involved in education as well as many other business and professional capacities. By becoming a unified body with the same goals and objectives—those being community service, education and cultural advancement—we can only serve our community better and uplift the name of Alpha Kappa Alpha. Our young people need role models to help guide and mold their lives toward positive goals and success. I also believe by serving AKA and the community, the lives of each member will be greatly enriched. I believe having a chapter in this community will serve as a strong force for positive change." Karen was right in that Phi Mu Omega has established itself as a presence for community service, promoting education and cultural advancement, and as a force for positive change. As a result, the communities served are better for it and the lives of members are enriched.

Charter Secretary Lorraine wrote in 1999, ". . . I honestly feel that with the right leadership, a chapter in this location could be very dynamic and could have a significant effect on the communities represented and served. For this and other reasons, I strongly support an active graduate chapter in McComb." In 2013, she reflected, "I am convinced that Phi Mu Omega has significantly impacted numerous girls and women as well as communities through its outstanding service programs, community outreach activities, and positive publicity throughout Southwest Mississippi. Many people recognize the pink and green and know that it represents class and extraordinary service. Our presence in Southwest Mississippi is well-documented in the local news media, contrary to that of several other service or civic organizations. I expect the presence, publicity, and the power of Alpha Kappa Alpha to continue for eternity in Southwest Mississippi."

Charter Financial Secretary Mary Helena wrote in 1999, "Upon graduating from ASU, I became focused solely on maintaining a family and career, with a plan to continue membership as an active member . . . . Unfortunately, my plan to remain active had to be postponed, mainly due to there not being a nearby chapter available. For years, I have longed to be an active member of the sorority to which I belong. Now, upon finding a group of ladies with the common interest of establishing a new chapter . . . to serve the counties of Amite, Lincoln, and Pike, I can fulfill my wish. Together, we can continue to use our leadership abilities, fellowship, and scholarship to serve our communities. We can accomplish this, and so much more, if we are granted the privilege of becoming a chapter." In 2013, she reflected, "I am so proud to be an active Alpha Kappa Alpha Phi Mu Omega member. I love participating in the many service projects, through our new global initiatives of our Sorority. It makes me even prouder when I see the smiles, love, and appreciation of the recipients of our chapter's services. When I attend functions of the Sorority, I love to interact with other members in my region. I wish I could attend them all. My life has been enriched. I held several offices in my chapter, including financial secretary, hostess, doorkeeper, and corresponding secretary. It is in my future to become a "Golden" member while still providing service to all mankind. There is no other like our sisterhood. I had the pleasure of pinning my daughter and my niece. I look forward to pinning my youngest granddaughter who is now 4!"

Marcia opined in 1999 that, ". . . There are only a few organizations in our community that are trying to meet the needs of many people and with our Sorority, we can aid in the betterment of our people and community. Another reason is that the Sorority can aid in the advancement of our heritage. We must believe that a higher being has put us together to do some of these marvelous works. Our Sorority can only grow with hard work and dedication." Thirteen years later she stated, "Phi Mu Omega has impacted many communities and families since its inception in 2000. The chapter tries to implement programs according to guidelines that benefit our geographical area . . . . Our chapter wins a gold medal for captivating educators, current and retired; those are hard workers who realize that young adults are our future. My prayers for Phi Mu Omega are to keep pushing. Time and membership change, but Alpha Kappa Alpha remains the same." Amen!!

CHAPTER IV

INTERNATIONAL AND REGIONAL PERSPECTIVES

International

A Legacy of Sisterhood and Timeless Service

Confined to what she called "a small circumscribed life" in the segregated and male-dominated milieu that characterized the early 1900s, Howard University co-ed Ethel Hedgeman dreamed of creating a support network for women with like minds coming together for mutual uplift, and coalescing their talents and strengths for the benefit of others. In 1908, her vision crystallized as Alpha Kappa Alpha, the first Negro Greek-letter sorority. Five years later (1913), lead incorporator Nellie Quander ensured Alpha Kappa Alpha's perpetuity through incorporation in the District of Columbia.

Together with eight other coeds at the mecca for Negro education, Hedgeman crafted a design that not only fostered interaction, stimulation, and ethical growth among members; but also provided hope for the masses. From the core group of nine at Howard, AKA has grown into a force of more than 265,000 collegiate members and alumnae, constituting 972 chapters in 42 states, the District of Columbia, the US Virgin Islands, the Bahamas, Germany, South Korea, Japan, Liberia, and Canada.

Because they believed that Negro college women represented "the highest—more education, more enlightenment, and more of almost everything that the great mass of Negroes never had—Hedgeman and her cohorts worked to honor what she called "an everlasting debt to raise them (Negroes) up and to make them better." For more than a century, the Alpha Kappa Alpha

Sisterhood has fulfilled that obligation by becoming an indomitable force for good in their communities, state, nation, and the world.

The Alpha Kappa Alpha program today still reflects the communal consciousness steeped in the

AKA tradition and embodied in AKA's credo, "To be supreme in service to all mankind."

Cultural awareness and social advocacy marked Alpha Kappa Alpha's infancy, but within one year (1914) of acquiring corporate status, AKA had also made its mark on education, establishing a scholarship award. The programming was a prelude to the thousands of pioneering and enduring initiatives that eventually defined the Alpha Kappa Alpha brand.

Through the years, Alpha Kappa Alpha has used the Sisterhood as a grand lever to raise the status of African-Americans, particularly girls and women. AKA has enriched minds and encouraged life-long learning; provided aid for the poor, the sick, and underserved; initiated social action to advance human and civil rights; worked collaboratively with other groups to maximize outreach on progressive endeavors; and continually produced leaders to continue its credo of service.

Guided by twenty-eight international presidents from Nellie M. Quander (1913-1919) to Carolyn House Stewart (2010-2014), with reinforcement from a professional headquarters staff since 1949; AKA's corps of volunteers has instituted groundbreaking social action initiatives and social service programs that have timelessly transformed communities for the better—continually emitting progress in cities, states, the nation, and the world.

Signal Program Initiatives

2000s—Launched Emerging Young Leaders, a bold move to prepare 10,000 girls in grades 6-8 to excel as young leaders equipped to respond to the challenges of the 21st century; initiated homage for civil rights milestones by honoring the Little Rock Nine's 1957

desegregation of Central High (Little Rock, Ar.) following the Supreme Court's 1954 decision declaring segregated schools unconstitutional; donated $1 million to Howard University to fund scholarships and preserve Black culture (2008); strengthened the reading skills of 16,000 children through a $1.5 million after school demonstration project in low-performing, economically deprived, inner city schools (2002); and improved the quality of life for people of African descent through continuation of aid to African countries.

1990s—Built 10 schools in South Africa (1998); added the largest number of minorities to the National Bone Marrow Registry (1996); Became first civilian organization to create memorial to World War II unsung hero Dorie Miller (1991).

1980s—Adopted more than 27 African villages, earning Africare's 1986 Distinguished Service Award; encouraged awareness of and participation in the nation's affairs, registering more than 350, 000 new voters; and established the Alpha Kappa Alpha Educational Advancement Foundation (1981), a multi-million dollar entity that annually awards more than $100,000 in scholarships, grants, and fellowships.

1970s—Was only sorority to be named an inaugural member of Operation Big Vote (1979); completed pledge of one-half million to the United Negro College Fund (1976); and purchased Dr. Martin Luther King's boyhood home for the MLK Center for Social Change (1972).

1960s—Sponsored inaugural Domestic Travel Tour, a one-week cultural excursion for 30 high school students (1969); launched a "Heritage Series" on African-American achievers (1965); and emerged as the first women's group to win a grant to operate a federal job corps center (1965), preparing youth 16-21 to function in a highly competitive economy.

1950s—Promoted investing in Black businesses by depositing initial $38,000 for AKA Investment Fund with the first and only Negro firm on Wall Street (1958). Spurred Sickle Cell Disease research and education with grants to Howard Hospital and publication of The Sickle Cell Story (1958).

1940s—Invited other Greek-letter organizations to come together to establish the American Council on Human Rights to empower racial uplift and economic development (1948); Acquired observer status from the United Nations (1946); and challenged the absence of people of color from pictorial images used by the government to portray Americans (1944).

1930s—Became first organization to take out NAACP life membership (1939); Created nation's first Congressional lobby that impacted legislation on issues ranging from decent living conditions and jobs to lynching (1938); and established the nation's first mobile health clinic, providing relief to 15,000 Negroes plagued by famine and disease in the Mississippi Delta (1935).

1920s—Worked to dispel notions that Negroes were unfit for certain professions, and guided Negroes in avoiding career mistakes (1923); pushed anti-lynching legislation (1921).

1900s—Promoted Negro culture and encouraged social action through presentation of Negro artists and social justice advocates, including elocutionist Nathaniel Guy, Hull House founder Jane Addams, and U. S. Congressman Martin Madden (1908-1915). Established the first organizational scholarship at Howard University (1914).

Earnestine Green McNealey, Ph.D., AKA Historian
August 2013

Regional Perspective

South Eastern Region

A Legacy of Sisterhood and Timeless Service

The expansion of Alpha Kappa Alpha Sorority in the 1920s created a need for close supervision of chapters. The Boule, the governing body, responded by grouping chapters into regions and providing for the election of regional directors. Emerging from the Southern Region, which included the states of Texas, Alabama, Tennessee, Mississippi, and Arkansas in 1925, the South Eastern Region now includes the states of Alabama, Tennessee and Mississippi, often dubbed the ATM by the 24th regional director.

With an active membership of almost six thousand in 104 chapters (57 graduate and 47 undergraduate), the South Eastern Region ranks fifth among the ten Alpha Kappa Alpha regions. To some extent, its rank was determined by a series of re-alignments, the largest of which was approved by the 1953 Boule and implemented at a joint conference with the South Atlantic Region. That joint conference was held April 15-18, 1954, on the campus of Alabama A&M College (now Alabama A&M University) at Normal, AL.

Although the 1925 Constitution provided for regional conferences in April of each year, "if possible," the South Eastern Region held its first regional conference in 1933 with Carolyn Blanton, the second Regional Director, presiding. Alpha Delta Omega, Pi, and Alpha Psi Chapters of Nashville, TN, were the host chapters. Since then, there have been eighty-one additional regional conferences.

Ironically, the presence of Alpha Kappa Alpha at Historically Black Colleges and Universities (HBCUs) was initially delayed. The AKA Standards Committee's refusal to recommend the chartering of chapters on campuses without "A" ratings from national or regional agencies was a main reason for the delay. Another reason was the reluctance of HBCU administrators to permit the establishment of "secret societies" on their campuses. Pi, the region's oldest chapter, was chartered at Meharry Medical College in 1921. A mixed chapter comprised of undergraduates and graduates, it was moved to Fisk University in 1927, with the approval of the Boule and Fisk administrators. Early on, administrators had not allowed the chartering of fraternities and sororities at Fisk. Alpha Delta Omega was chartered for graduates at Nashville that same year. By the end of the twenties, only one additional undergraduate chapter—Chi at Talladega College (1924)-had been chartered in the region as we know it today. By 1930, three graduate chapters existed within the boundaries of the present South Eastern Region: Omicron Omega at Birmingham, AL (1924), Pi Omega at Chattanooga, TN (1925), and Alpha Pi Omega at Knoxville, TN (1929).

The South Eastern Region has contributed tremendously to the leadership of Alpha Kappa Alpha. Three Regional Directors advanced to the office of Supreme Basileus. Maude Brown Porter, the seventh Supreme Basileus, served from 1931 to 1933. Called the catalyst for the Mississippi Health Project, she stressed the need for quality programs and advocated high scholastic achievement. Arnetta G. Wallace, fifth Regional Director, became the fourteenth Supreme Basileus in 1953 and served until 1958. She established the first international chapter (Liberia) and commissioned and presented the first official history of Alpha Kappa Alpha. Julia Brogdon Purnell completed her tenure as Regional Director in 1962 and served as Supreme Basileus from 1962 to 1966. She secured a $4 million contract from the U.S. Government to operate the Cleveland Job Corps Center and held the first International Undergraduate Leadership School.

Three Supreme Basilei were born in the South Eastern Region: Bobbie Beatrix Scott (1927-1929); Ida Jackson (1933 to 1936); and Eva Lois Evans (1994-1998). Scott, who worked for a National Headquarters and developed a plan to include undergraduates in directorate proceedings, was born in Vicksburg, MS. Jackson, known best as founder of the Mississippi Health Project, was also born in Vicksburg. She was responsible for expanding Alpha Kappa Alpha to the West Coast. Evans, 24th Supreme Basileus, was born in Memphis, TN. She served as First Supreme Anti-Basileus, Great Lakes Regional Director, and International Program Chairman before her elevation to AKA's highest office. PIMS (Partnership in Science and Mathematics) was her signature program.

AKA Founder Harriet Terry, who taught English at Alabama A& M College for 37 years, was a charter member of Epsilon Gamma Omega Chapter. Mayme Williams, fifth Regional Director, was elected First Supreme Anti-Basileus and consequently served as Chairman of the National Health Committee. Mary M. Chambers of Normal, AL, was also elected First Supreme Anti-Basileus. She played a major role in securing the $4 million Job Corps award, wrote a series of how-to-books, served as International Program Chairman and Undergraduate Program Advisor.

Four Executive Directors have had ties to the South Eastern Region: Carey Preston, a native of Columbus, MS, and the longest-serving Director (1949-1974); Earnestine Green McNealey (1980-1985); Emma Lily Henderson (1997-1998); and Cynthia Howell, recently appointed. McNealey currently lives in Tuscaloosa, AL, and is affiliated with Eta Xi Omega Chapter. Henderson is a native of Birmingham, AL; Howell formerly resided in Tuskegee and Huntsville, AL, and she was affiliated with Epsilon Gamma Omega Chapter.

As Chairman of the International Program Committee, Juanita Sims Doty was instrumental in securing a $1.5 million grant for an after-school reading program, the Ivy Reading AKAdemy. Countless other South Eastern members have chaired committees and served unstintingly at all levels of the sorority.

South Eastern chapters have always embraced Alpha Kappa Alpha programs. Geographic boundaries have shifted as the region evolved, but the mission remains the same: "to be of service to all mankind." From Maude Brown Porter, the first Regional Director, to Adrienne P-K Washington, the 24th, visionary, creative leaders have given timeless service and inspired other Alpha Kappa Alpha women to serve unselfishly. From early cultural and social involvement to the current Emerging Young Leaders program (EYL), the "Sophisticated Sorors of the South Eastern Region" have improved their communities by designing and employing effective service programs and initiatives.

Timeless Programs and Initiatives

1920s—Observed Founders' Day; developed social and cultural programs.

1930s—Was the site of the Mississippi Health Project; conducted social and cultural programs.

1940s—Introduced Fashionetta® to Alpha Kappa Alpha as a creative fundraiser; sponsored cultural programs; engaged in political advocacy.

1950s—Operated the Tuskegee Gift Shop, coordinated by Beta Xi Omega Chapter and funded in collaboration with other chapters to provide free gift shopping for veterans at the VA Hospital at Tuskegee, AL; sponsored health projects.

1960s—Participated in the Civil Rights Movement; conducted tutorial programs; developed local Black heritage programs.

1970s—Sponsored reading programs; presented local Black History programs; recruited and mentored participants for the AKA Domestic Travel Tour, a one-week cultural excursion; distributed the AKA Heritage Series, which showcases African American women in professional careers; gave awards for most creative use of the Series.

1980s—Adopted more than 20 HBCUs and presented checks to college and university presidents at the sorority's 1990 Boule; adopted African villages to address drought, starvation and their attendant problems through Africare; established a $10,000 endowed regional scholarship in memory of Harriet Terry; supported the Cleveland Job Corps through its Shower of Love initiative; recruited participants for the AKA Leadership Fellows program; gave chapter scholarships; conducted mentoring programs for Girls Inc. and similar groups.

1990s—Developed Ivy AKAdemies, comprehensive learning centers; received motivational awards for six model AKAdemies; partnered with Piney Woods Country Life School to conduct a regional residential summer math and science camp for 30 middle school students; replicated the Piney Woods model at two additional sites; was the first AKA region to build a school in South Africa; organized chapter foundations.

2000s—Launched Emerging Young Leaders, an AKA initiative to equip girls in grades 6-8 to meet the challenges of the 21st century; conducted a Girl's Youth Summit at the 81st and 82nd South Eastern

Regional Conferences; contributed winning student essays to the Young Authors publication; erected a marker honoring Honorary Member Rosa Parks in collaboration with Alpha Kappa Alpha, Inc. and the city of Montgomery; facilitated the unveiling of a landmark in Mound Bayou, MS, to commemorate the Mississippi Health Project; shared a $1.5 million AKA grant from the U.S. Department of Education to strengthen reading skills at nine demonstration sites, including one at Birmingham, AL, administered by Omicron Omega Chapter and another at Jackson, MS, administered by Beta Delta Chapter; facilitated construction of a Habitat for Humanity house for a family whose home was destroyed by Hurricane Katrina; hosted the AKA Centennial Traveling Exhibit at Memphis, TN (Beta Epsilon Omega Chapter), in 2008; contributed more than $400,000 to 28 HBCUs in the South Eastern Region; announced that 13 regional endowed scholarships have been capitalized with $20,000 or more in their AKA Educational Advancement Foundation accounts; acknowledged recognition of Unsung AKA Heroes of the Civil Rights Movement; conducted Youth Financial Literacy Campaigns; volunteered more than 200,000 hours of service, benefiting 1.8 million people and contributing more than $1.6 million to communities in the South Eastern Region in 2003-2004, a typical year of service in the South Eastern Region.

Mattie Daniels Thomas, Ph.D.
AKA Historian, South Eastern Region
September 2013

Chapter V

OTHER CHAPTERS

Alcorn State University, an HBCU in Lorman, MS (Claiborne County), is the only four-year college located in Southwest Mississippi.

However, when Gayden went to Purdue University as a Graduate Teaching Assistant in the fall of 1969, to her delight an interest group was in the making. Purdue was a state university which had only recently admitted black students. In 1969, approximately 2% of the student population was African-American. It should go without saying that Gayden was the only one in her graduate classes. The young ladies had a strong determination and a passion for progression because there were so few African-Americans there. There was a definite need for the sisterhood. Following the required procedures and regulations, the first undergraduate chapter of Alpha Kappa Alpha was finalized. As a graduate member who was still active, Gayden participated in the charter initiation of twelve undergrads into Epsilon Rho chapter on December 13, 1969, on the Lafayette, Indiana, campus. The twelve extraordinary women who chartered Epsilon Rho recognized the need and worked hard to bring the presence of Alpha Kappa Alpha to the Purdue campus. They filled a void in the campus community with the sisterhood, leadership, scholarship, and service that Alpha Kappa Alpha provided. Gayden cannot remember the name of the other graduate members who were the actual sponsors, but she does remember having a wonderful time with the undergraduate members. They were Ladys Barlow, Phyllis Johnson, Marshenell Conley, Betty Poindexter, Vicki Epps, Carolyn Ross, Pamela Ford, Harriet Scott, Jane Hart, Catherine Tompkins, Cheryl Jackson, and Camilla Ware. Gayden especially remembers Epps, the tall, fair-skinned, curly-headed lady from Indianapolis and has tried several times to locate her through her once Regional Director and now International Vice President Dorothy Buckhanan Wilson. As far as Gayden has been able to determine, the chapter was dissolved after about forty (40) years on the campus. Gayden has made several contacts with campus representatives of Greek organizations but has received no response from any Epsilon Rho member. According to a posting on a current website (Http://web.ics.purdue.edu/akaep/), ". . . The lovely ladies of the Epsilon Rho chapter have upheld the prominent reputation of being a community leadership driven and socially conscious organization for forty years . . ." It further invites visitors to "sign the guest book and check the calendar for upcoming events," but the original website at akaep08@yahoo.com provides no additional information. Based on the most recent information Gayden has obtained, the chapter ceased to exist in 2008. A picture from the website shows only the original members, and no listing for the chapter appears in the chapter directory on the official Alpha Kappa Alpha website.

Lillie Turner (now deceased) was a charter member of Xi Mu Omega chapter in Columbia, MS, before becoming a charter member of Phi Mu Omega. She is the only member of this chapter to hold the distinction of being a charter member of two chapters!

Claudia Russell Moore, a life member, joined the chapter in 2007, after relocating from the Chicago-land area following her retirement to be close to her mother who lived in Mississippi. Moore was a charter member of Xi Nu Omega (chartered July 1982), one of several graduate chapters in the metropolitan Chicago area.

CHAPTER VI

CHAPTER PRESIDENTS
(2000-2014)

2000-2001

Betty Spann Wilson-McSwain

In the year of Phi Mu Omega's chartering, the nation was in the midst of a fundamental change in ideology with the installation of George W. Bush, a Republican Texas billionaire from a prominent political family, as President. His election signaled an end to the concerns of middle class and poor families from that of the previous presidential administration. President Bush and the congress would probably implement austerity measures which could negatively impact people of color, other minorities, the poor, and especially African-Americans. The relative economic prosperity of the Clinton years would soon become a nostalgic reminiscence.

Regional Director Pettway might have thought about that when she appointed Betty as the charter president. Through various conversations and interactions, Pettway knew that Betty would make sure that Phi Mu Omega got off to a great start. Chapter members are grateful to Pettway for having the foresight to give that chapter a determined, fearless, and resolute leader. Bringing women together from five counties who had families, careers, other civic affiliations, and unique personalities required a strong and knowledgeable leader. Betty had the intensity, dynamic personality, and commanding presence that could motivate others to get things done, and the chapter accomplished much during her administration.

With Supreme President Dr. Norma Solomon White at the helm with her ON TRACK program, chapter members quickly got on board and initiated community service projects which will be detailed later. Initiated into Gamma Omicron chapter at Tougaloo College in 1986, Betty served as Vice President and President of her undergraduate chapter. She and Phi Mu Omega charter Vice President Karen Bryant (Luckett) were co-initiates in Gamma Omicron. She graduated from Tougaloo in 1989 with a B. S. degree in Physics.

Betty is the third of five children born to George and Ruby Spann. A native of Jackson, Betty has two sisters and two brothers. She attended the Jackson Public Schools and graduated from Callaway High in 1985, where she was a Top Ten Scholar, a Hall of Fame inductee, and captain of the flag corps and volleyball team. Betty also played basketball, was a member of the National Honor Society, Mu Alpha Theta (a math society), and the safety club. She was Student Body Vice-President during her senior year and served as president of the Future Business Leaders of America. She placed first as Miss Future Business Leader of America for the State of Mississippi and represented the state at the national competition.

Betty taught in Clarksdale, MS, and Helena-West Helena, Arkansas, and obtained her master's and educational specialist's degrees in Educational Leadership from Delta State University and Mississippi College respectively before coming to the McComb School District as an assistant principal at McComb High School. After several years as assistant principal, she became the Business and Technology Complex Director and currently is the District's Director of Curriculum and Federal Programs. Betty is in the final phase of completing her doctoral degree in Educational Leadership at Mississippi College with her dissertation research centered on the acquisition of early literacy skills.

Married to Larry McSwain, she has one son (Darrian Wilson), one stepson (Trey Javen Wilson), and four stepdaughters. Though she resides in Brookhaven, Betty attends Mizpeh Full Gospel Church in Magnolia, MS. She said she is "grateful for the opportunity to serve God through the vehicle of Alpha Kappa Alpha."

Betty's knowledge is invaluable to Phi Mu Omega and she has served in many other capacities besides Charter President. She was Secretary, Parliamentarian, and Assistant Secretary. She has chaired the Connections and Bylaws committees and served on numerous other committees during her tenure with the chapter. She also served as Cluster IV Coordinator for the South Eastern Region in 2002 and 2003 and workshop convener at several South Eastern Regional Conferences. She was recognized as a "Silver Star" at the 79th South Eastern Regional Conference in Birmingham.

Although Ivy Omega Interest Group participated in Relay for Life and held a New Year's Ball in 1999, Phi Mu Omega began its Relay for Life and its Annual Scholarship Ball signature programs under Betty's leadership. "Jazz by the Lake," another chapter signature fundraiser, was the brainchild of Betty.

Celia Pearson joined the chapter immediately following the chartering reception and chapter membership began to grow during Betty's presidency (see appendix for list of members for 2000-2001).

2002-2003

Karen Bryant Luckett, DMD

Karen ascended to the office of President during the Mississippi Governorship of Kirk Fordice, a wealthy Vicksburg construction company owner who was a fierce fiscal conservative. He had a reputation for his toughness and his gruff, direct manner of speaking. Karen's personality was a sharp contrast to that of Governor Fordice's. She brought a soft but effective tone to Phi Mu Omega. Perhaps, she knew that our children's futures were not guaranteed in the realm of public and higher education because neither the Statehouse nor the legislature was in the mood to give anybody anything! Karen presided over the chapter's first Membership Intake Process. Karen was also the first chapter member to attend a Leadership Seminar.

Officers who served with Karen were Vice President Lorraine B. Gayden, Secretary Frances Hogan, Assistant Secretary Marcia Leonard, Treasurer

Celia Pearson, Financial Secretary Margaret Therrell, Corresponding Secretary Nikki Beckley-Holloway, *Ivy Leaf* Reporter Julia Parker, Hostess Mary Helena Thompson, Doorkeeper Zelphia Taylor, Historian Nancy Denham, Chaplain Monesa Watts, and Custodian Nikki (see roster in appendix for membership in 2002 and 2003).

Karen was the second child born to Elnora Nelson Bryant and the late Percy Bryant. Her father's brother the late Curtis Conway Bryant ("C.C.") was a civil rights pioneer in McComb, Pike County, and the state of Mississippi, serving as local branch president of the NAACP and in several positions at the state level. His relentless fight for justice and equality in Pike County was cause for alarm for his family, his neighborhood, and his church. He has a storied history with the NAACP, and the annual C. C. Bryant Memorial Award is presented each year in McComb at the annual Martin Luther King Day celebration. Karen grew up with this fierce freedom fighter in her presence and on her mind. "C.C." was charter member Cynthia Bryant's grandfather.

Karen was a precocious child (her mother was a high school English teacher before leaving the profession to work in industry) who excelled in the sciences, so it was probable that she would choose a career in the medical profession. Karen, a 1983 McComb High School graduate, attended and graduated from Tougaloo College in 1987 with a B.S. degree in biology. She then enrolled at the University Of Mississippi School Of Dentistry in Jackson, a part of the University of Mississippi Medical Center (UMC). The University of Mississippi, or "Ole Miss" in Oxford, has an infamous past associated with the historic enrollment of James Meredith in 1962 which required the deployment of federal troops to insure his admission. Meredith was the first African-American graduate of Ole Miss. Karen earned her DMD in 1991 and received her dental licensure in 1992. She continued residency training in general practice at the UMC School of Dentistry in 1992 and 1993 followed by two years as an associate in the office of Marcus K. Jackson, DDS in Jackson until 1994.

In 1994 Karen moved back to McComb and established her private practice of general dentistry which has been in continuous operation since that time. She holds professional memberships in the American Dental Association, the Mississippi Dental Association, the National Dental Association, the Magnolia Dental Society, the American Association of Women Dentists, and the Mississippi Association of Women Dentists.

Locally, Karen was a board member of the Children's Advocacy Center (2001-2003) and a member of the former Pike County Minority Business League (2001-2004). In 2007, the Pike County Negro Business and Professional Women recognized Karen as a Woman of Distinction. She is a member of the Pike County Chamber of Commerce, which highlighted her practice as the "Business of the Month" in January 2012. She was inducted into the McComb High School Hall of Fame in 2013.

Karen is married to Paul D. Luckett, Esquire, formerly of Canton, MS.

Karen has served the chapter as Vice President, Corresponding secretary, hostess, parliamentarian, *Ivy Leaf* Reporter, and chairman of the Bylaws, Basilei Council, and Program committees.

Chilibra Patterson reactivated with the chapter in January 2002. Unfortunately, charter members Taylor and Bryant-Patterson became inactive that year, and Phi Mu Omega's membership dropped to 13. Fortunately, Phi Mu Omega conducted its first Membership Intake Process on November 7-9, 2003, and added eight new, wonderful women to the sisterhood. Initiates were Rolanda Michelle Bates, Tabitha Carr, Velma Dilworth, Madeleine Floyd, Sandra Isaac, Cora Shannon, Joyce Tillman, and Tammy Witherspoon, bringing the chapter's membership back up to 21 (see Chapter 7 for Significant Membership Changes).

2004-2005

Lorraine Banks Gayden

When Gayden assumed leadership of the chapter, George W. Bush had been re-elected President of the United States, so there was a general consensus to expect more of the same social insensitivity to poor and middle class families. To add to the problems, his "No Child Left Behind" Program was now the law of the land. Members had to focus on the proper and successful education of children for an uncertain future in a global economy. Education was always Gayden's passion, so her goal was to increase the amount and number of scholarships that Phi Mu Omega offered. The chapter successfully increased its scholarship awards, but has since had changes in the number and amount of scholarships awarded based on chapter membership and fundraising efforts.

The third president of Phi Mu Omega, Gayden had served as Charter Secretary. A 1969 graduate of Jackson State College (now University) in Jackson, MS, Lorraine became a member of Gamma Rho chapter on November 19, 1966, in the fall of her sophomore year. A native of McComb, MS, she had unsuccessfully tried to organize a graduate chapter in her hometown back in the early '70's with her biological sister Bobbie Banks and two other biological sisters Beverly Bates Nobles and Sonya Bates Norwood (Brandy and Ray J's mom) who were all members of the sorority. She had assisted in the chartering of undergraduate chapter Epsilon Rho at Purdue University in 1969 when she was a graduate student there.

Officers who served during this administration were vice president Frances Hogan, secretary Monesa Watts, assistant secretary Betty Wilson, treasurer Margaret Therrell, financial secretary Celia Pearson, corresponding secretary Mary Helena Thompson, *Ivy Leaf* Reporter Nikki Beckley-Holloway, hostess Nancy Denham, historian Marcia Leonard, doorkeeper Julia Parker, parliamentarian Karen Luckett, and chaplain Doris Jacques (see membership roster in appendix for chapter members in 2004 and 2005).

Born in McComb on October 21, 1947, to Prentiss Banks, Sr. and Lela Wells Banks, Lorraine is the eldest of three children—one brother and one sister—who became a member of Gamma Rho chapter in the fall of 1966. She was considered a "nerd" by her siblings because she read by the streetlight when their mother cut the lights off at night in the bedroom she shared with her sister Bobbie. She was studious and among the older members—age-wise and sorority-wise.

Lorraine attended the McComb Public Schools, which were then certainly "separate but *unequal.*" Nevertheless, she is proud of the education she received at Burglund High School where she ranked third of 116 students in the graduating class of 1965. She was competitive and extremely conscientious about social conditions and the world in general. As a result, she took part in the student walkout at the school as a freshman in October of 1961 to protest the expulsion of two students for participating in sit-ins at the local Greyhound Bus Station. Following her sophomore and junior years at Burglund, Jackson State University (JSU) selected her to attend the Continuing Education Enrichment Program (CEEP) for eight weeks and the College Readiness Program on the college campus following her senior year, so by the time she actually enrolled at Jackson State, she really knew her way around campus! She finished her coursework for a B.A. degree in English in December 1968 and returned to march with her class in May 1969. Thankfully, neither her undergraduate degree nor her advanced degrees cost her parents any money.

During her years at Burglund, she was President of the Future Homemakers of America. Imagine the irony of that—she wanted to be a college professor—not a homemaker! She was active in the French Club and various extracurricular activities such as the school chorus, her church's Sunday school and youth choir, and the Girl Scouts. She began piano lessons in the 5th grade and abandoned them during her senior year. However, during high school she played for a Senior Choir at a local church and for the youth choir at her church and earned extra spending money to buy fancy school clothes.

During her tenure at JSU, a panel selected her to participate in the Harvard-Yale-Columbia Intensive Summer Studies Program (ISSP) at Columbia following her sophomore year (1967) and at Yale following her junior year (1968). It was during those summers that "I received confirmation that I could compete with students anywhere," she said. Following her nomination as a Woodrow Wilson Fellow, Purdue offered her a Graduate Teaching Assistantship. She earned her M.A. in English from Purdue in 1971 and her Educational Specialist degree in secondary education with an emphasis in English from the University of Southern Mississippi in Hattiesburg, MS, in 1996.

Lorraine taught at Eva Gordon Attendance Center (now South Pike High School), Alcorn State University in Lorman, MS, and McComb High School. Her greatest achievement was being named the third African-American Director of a county Welfare Department in the State of Mississippi in 1981 and the first and only one in her home county of Pike to date. After 11 ½ years with the Department, she returned to teaching and retired from McComb High in 2002 after being honored as the Teacher of the Year at McComb High in 1991 and 2002 during her 14 years there.

She is a charter member of the Omicron Federated Club of McComb, an affiliate of the Mississippi and the National Association of Colored Women's Clubs, Inc., and Mission Pike County, an interracial and interdenominational organization dedicated to racial reconciliation in the body of Christ. She is on the Board of Directors of the McComb Interdenominational Care Association (MICA) and Pike County Habitat for Humanity. She also serves as President of the local McComb Association of Education Employees and youth advisor for the Omicron Pre-teen and Junior clubs.

In Phi Mu Omega, Lorraine has also served as vice president, *Ivy Leaf* Reporter, Historian, Bylaws Committee Chairman and chairman of the Standards Committee for the past eight years. Gayden was a co-recipient of the Vanessa Rogers Long Humanitarian Award at the 2011 South Eastern Regional Conference in Birmingham, AL.

Lorraine married her junior and senior year prom date Robert. They celebrated 42 years of marriage in 2013. They have one daughter Robin Elaine Gayden Johnson Alexander, one granddaughter Lauren Johnson, and one grandson William Robert Alexander.

2006-2009

Frances Bennett Hogan

While "W" was still the president during most of her presidency, Frances' term was marked by a historical event of extraordinary significance—the election of the first African-American President in the history of the United States of America. Like Barack Obama, Frances made history in Phi Mu Omega by being the first president to serve consecutive terms. She was responsible for expanding the chapter's scholarship assistance program to include the nontraditional graduate—a GED recipient. She was the charter hostess and had served as assistant secretary and secretary, *Ivy Leaf* reporter, and vice president before becoming president. She has also chaired the Program and Sisterly Relations committees. The chapter's biannual signature Student Leadership Conference and "Jazz by the Lake" events began under her leadership. Under Francis' leadership, the chapter purchased its lighted "20 Pearls" board and held its second Membership Intake Process.

Officers who served with Frances were vice president Nikki Beckley-Holloway, secretary Betty Wilson, assistant secretary Joyce Tillman, treasurer Tabitha Carr, financial secretary Nancy Denham, corresponding secretary Madeleine Floyd, hostess Karen Bryant Luckett, *Ivy Leaf* Reporter Lorraine B. Gayden, doorkeeper Mary Helena Thompson, and chaplain Velma Dilworth (see roster in appendix for membership during 2006-2009).

The chapter's second Membership Intake Program in 2007 took place in Magnolia, MS, at the minority-owned bed-and-breakfast Magnolia Terrace with Celia Pearson serving as Membership chairman. Phi Mu Omega added thirteen members: Janis Anderson, Sheanda Davis, Robin Tyler Faust, Kayla Dixon Freeman, Ruby Husband, Mashanda Lee (Thomas), Shirlene Lowery, Janice Samuels, Sheila Sartin, Juanita Steptoe, and Vanessa Wilbert, and two legacies Alfonda Hogan Powell and Mary Elizabeth Tillman (see Significant Membership Changes in chapter VII for details). Several other reactivations and changes occurred during Francis' terms, but at one point membership reached an all-time high of 43!!

Born Frances Bennett on March 4th in McComb, Pike County, MS, to proud parents the late Hiram and Marcella Bennett, she is the youngest of **14** children—seven boys and seven girls! Francis was the second of her siblings to earn a college degree. She attended the McComb Public Schools and graduated from Higgins High School in 1969. She earned her B.S.degree in Business Education from Alcorn State University in 1974. At Alcorn, she became a member of Gamma Phi chapter in 1971. While there, she also met and later married Alvin Hogan of Shreveport, LA. They have one daughter, legacy member Alfonda Felicia Renee Westbrook, one son Joseph Lydell, a granddaughter Kirsten, and two grandsons, Eric and Kaleb.

Before entering the teaching profession in 2001, she had worked in the private sector for a manufacturing company as an administrative assistant for 24 years. There, she developed skills that would prove to be beneficial to her in her next career as a teacher—lots of patience and compassion. Since coming into the education profession, Frances returned to school and acquired her M.S. degree in Special

Education from Alcorn State in 2002 and a M.A. in Supervision and Administration from the University of Phoenix in 2010. She then completed study in education at Nova University.

Frances and her husband are active members of St. Catherine Spiritual Church in McComb, where she has served as a Sunday school teacher, usher, and choir member. She currently serves as a church mother and the church clerk. She is also a member of the Baertown Improvement Organization, the Adult Education Literacy Program, and a former NAACP member. One of her proudest moments was her selection as the *"2006 Mother of the Year"* by the McComb *Enterprise-Journal.* Her picture and a full feature-length article appeared on the "More" page on Sunday, May 14th. She was named "Teacher of the Year" at the McComb Business and Technology during the 2003-2004 year, and students there selected her as "Parent of the Year" during the 2008-2009 school term.

It is her life's mission to make a difference in the lives of others just by giving. A favorite quote of hers by George Washington Carver is, "How far you go in life depends on you being tender with the young, compassionate with the aged, sympathetic with the striving and tolerant of the weak and the strong because someday in life you will have been all of these."

2010-2011

Nikkitta "Nikki" Nikole Beckley-Holloway

One year after Barack Obama's historic election, the chapter elected "Nikki" to lead Phi Mu Omega as Obama would lead the nation and the world. African-Americans were extremely proud and feeling "blessed and highly favored" by the Lord. Generally, Phi Mu Omega was feeling the euphoria as well and looking forward to "good times."

Nikki brought a lot of financial knowledge and a hands-on approach to the chapter. She was quite studious and kept abreast of all national policy and changes. A breast cancer survivor, Nikki leads the chapter in fundraising for its annual Relay for Life signature program and is an ardent supporter of chapter Breast Cancer Awareness activities.

Officers who served with Nikki were vice president Marcia Leonard, Secretary Tammy Witherspoon, assistant secretary Ruby Husband, financial secretary Claudia Moore, corresponding secretary Karen Luckett, hostess Vanessa Wilbert, *Ivy Leaf* Reporter Madeleine Floyd, doorkeeper Barbara Scott, parliamentarian Julia Parker, chaplain Doris Jacques, historian Lorraine B. Gayden, and custodian Frances Hogan.

At the end of 2010, several members from the Jackson area left Phi Mu Omega to join chapters closer to home or to become general members (See member roster in appendix for 2010-2011 membership).

Nikki is the only child born to Mr. and Mrs. Dennis Beckley of Hazlehurst, MS, in Copiah County. As such, many would think she is spoiled, but she is a smart, take-charge woman who knows how to handle her business.

Nikki was a 1997 initiate into Theta Sigma Omega chapter in Hattiesburg, MS. She was President of the Ivy Omega Interest Group which preceded Phi Mu Omega and served as the charter treasurer. Since that time, Nikki has held many positions in the chapter, including vice president, secretary, assistant secretary, corresponding secretary, and custodian. She has also served as chairman of the Program, Technology, Sisterly Relations, and Budget and Finance committees.

Nikki attended the Copiah County schools, graduating from Crystal Springs High School in 1987. She enrolled at the University of Southern Mississippi in Hattiesburg and earned a B.S. degree in Business Administration with an emphasis in accounting in 1990. She later earned a Master of Business Administration (MBA) from Mississippi College in Clinton, MS, in 1993. With these business and hands-on skills, she secured employment in the field of accounting for 18 years with the Copiah County Board of Supervisors, the Mississippi Department of Finance and Administration, the Mississippi Department of Education, the Mississippi State Auditor's Office and the Hazlehurst City Schools, where she served as Business Manager for the school district in her native county at the time of the chapter's chartering.

After fulfilling her chosen career path, she sought God's career path and was inspired to become a teacher. In 2009, she successfully completed the Mississippi Alternate Path to Quality Teachers Program through the Mississippi Community College Foundation. She is presently a teacher in the Brookhaven School District at Alexander Junior High School.

Nikki is the wife of Dexter and the mother of Dorian and Miles Holloway. She and her family are active members of Bethel African Methodist Episcopal Church in Brookhaven, MS, where they reside. She has served as a Stewardess, Sunday school teacher, and vacation Bible school instructor. She is currently a member of the Julia Haywood Missionary Society and the Wednesday Bible study group.

Serving the community is a vital part of Nikki's life; therefore, she served as President of the Parent-Teacher Association at Mamie Martin Elementary School and the Alexander Junior High Athletic Booster Club. She was a member of the NAACP and the Brookhaven Elementary PTA. She is currently a member of the Lipsey Middle School PTA, the Brookhaven High School Band Booster Club, the Brookhaven Greek Council, the Alcorn State University National Alumni Association, and a volunteer for Habitat for Humanity and the American Cancer Society. In her leisure time, she does private tutoring, but reading is her leisure-time passion.

2012—

Marcia Scott Leonard

Marcia's election as president came as President Obama was mounting his challenge for a second term as President of the United States. He had successfully made The Affordable Care Act the law of the land during his first term. The wind was at his and Marcia's backs. There was no stopping either of them from accomplishing their goals. Marcia was one of two members who first met on July 19, 1998, in McComb to discuss the possibility of chartering a graduate chapter in the McComb area. She was a charter member of Phi Mu Omega in 2000. During her term as *Ivy Leaf* reporter, she initiated and maintained an awesome chapter scrapbook long after her tenure ended as reporter. As vice president she was a dedicated program chairman. As president, Marcia brought a serious work ethic and a much-needed sense of humor to the chapter.

Officers who served with Marcia were vice president Ruby Husband, secretary Tammy Witherspoon, assistant secretaries Nikki Beckley-Holloway and Betty Wilson, treasurer Claudia Moore, financial secretary Madeleine Floyd, corresponding secretary Karen Bryant Luckett, hostess Mary Helena Thompson, doorkeeper Doris Jacques, *Ivy Leaf* Reporter Barbara Scott, chaplain Sheanda Davis, historian Lorraine B. Gayden (see member roster in appendix for membership during 2012-2013).

Prior to her tenure as chapter president, Marcia had served as vice president, secretary, *Ivy Leaf* Reporter, and historian. She had also chaired various committees, including Programs, Publicity, and Archives.

Marcia was born into a family with a well-known name. Rev. E.D. Scott was a minister and a presiding elder in the African Methodist Episcopal Church, and her mother Mary was an educator and minister of music throughout the McComb area as well as in Walthall County. Marcia and her twin sister were the seventh and eighth of a family of nine children. Because of her parents' influence, Marcia and her siblings grew up always playing an active role in the church and in the community.

Marcia was introduced to Alpha Kappa Alpha at an early age. Two of her older sisters had previously joined the sorority. In the Mississippi delta her sister Mary had become a charter member of the Epsilon Pi chapter established in 1969 at Mississippi Valley State University in Itta Bena. Her sister Etta had joined the Beta Psi chapter while attending Southern University in Baton Rouge, LA. Eighteen years later, Marcia followed in their footsteps. Pinned by their sister Mary, both Marcia and her twin sister Maria became members of the Epsilon Pi chapter at Mississippi Valley State University in the spring of 1986.

As Marcia continued her education, she transferred to another HBCU, Grambling State University in Grambling, LA, where she earned a B.S. degree in accounting. While she and her twin sister Maria were employed as accountants in the business office at Grambling, Marcia began work on her Master's degree in Business.

When Marcia relocated to McComb where teaching was the prominent profession, she learned that her degree in accounting made finding a job difficult. She commuted to Jackson, MS, where she worked as a head teller in the main office of Omni Bank. In McComb Marcia worked as a substitute teacher and attended William Carey College (now University) in Hattiesburg and earned her teaching credentials but realized that teaching was not her passion. According to Marcia, "The mission and everything else had changed so much since I went to school. I realized that my talents would not be best served in the field of education."

Marcia began working for Five County Child Development in Lawrence County as a payroll/accounting clerk. She was thankful that her work experience in the business office at Grambling State had prepared her for speedy work because at Five County she had to ensure accurate payroll for over 300 staff members at ten sites in the five counties!

In 2003, Marcia began work as an accountant with Faust and Associates, P.A., a CPA firm in McComb, MS. Marcia is currently employed with Faust where she has enjoyed her tenure for over ten years.

Marcia and her husband Anthony have enjoyed more than twenty years of marriage. Although they have no biological children, they have several God-children. Their youngest God-child, three-year old Kirsten is "truly a blessing from heaven." Marcia says, "She is so smart, I think she will be going to college when she is five."

In 1998, Marcia was one of the first sorors Doris Jacques called to discuss chartering a graduate chapter in the McComb area. Marcia was delighted because she had missed her sisterhood. When Marcia became a charter member of Phi Mu Omega chapter, she also became the second sister in her family to help charter a chapter of Alpha Kappa Alpha. Since becoming a member of Phi Mu Omega, Marcia has served in many capacities. In 2013 Marcia was instrumental in reactivating Sorors Dr. Lanasha Tanner, Katrina Sartin, and Sandra Pigott-Foxworth. In that same year, Marcia was re-elected to serve a second term as chapter president for 2014-2015.

CHAPTER VII

SIGNIFICANT MEMBERSHIP CHANGES

Lillie Mae Watson Turner
Ivy Beyond the Wall

The most devastating membership change occurred on March 26, 2001, a little over 14 months into the chapter's existence, when charter parliamentarian Lillie Mae Watson Turner passed away after a fairly short illness. Lillie had been unable to attend meetings for several months, but she had been a part of the group since 1999 when she served as secretary of the Ivy Omega Interest Group. Lillie, also a charter member of Xi Mu Omega in Columbia in 1980, was the only person in the chapter to hold such a distinction. A native of Lincoln County, Lillie was born to Mardessie Mae Watson and the late Willie Watson, Sr. She later moved to Brookhaven and united with the Center Street Church of Christ. She was an active member of the Bertha L. Johnson Federated Club, the Cole Lott Federated Club, the Ebonette Club, the Magnolia Region Counselors' Association, the MS School Counselors' Association, the MS Association of Multicultural Counseling and Development, MS Association of Educators, National Education Association, and the MS State Federation of Colored Women's and Youth Clubs, Inc. In 1995, she was selected as the "Mississippi Counselor of the Year." In 1996 the Brookhaven community recognized Lillie as an "Unsung Hero" for her many charitable club works and for dedicated and untiring service working with the youth of the community. She gave 30 years of service to the field of education. Lillie's many contributions made chapter members aware of the true meaning of "relay for life."

Lillie was an accomplished educator who had served as a teacher and counselor in the McComb, Brookhaven, and Copiah County school districts. In addition to her B.S. degree in elementary education from Jackson State University, she held a M.S. in guidance and counseling and a M.S. in administration and supervision from JSU. She later earned an Education Specialist degree in Counseling and Educational Psychology from the University of Southern Mississippi in Hattiesburg. She had taken additional courses towards a Ph. D.

Following her untimely demise, Phi Mu Omega members conducted the appropriate ceremony during visitation at Williams Mortuary in Brookhaven. Chapter members also attended and participated in the home going service at Center Street Church of Christ in Brookhaven. In her honor, the chapter initiated and continues to award annually the Lillie M. Turner Memorial Scholarship.

Another membership change was the Membership Intake Process. This process sanctioned by the Regional Director and the International Board of Directors is the recognized vehicle for adding significant numbers of members to existing chapters. Fortunately, Phi Mu Omega received permission for its two requests for approval to date.

A significant membership change occurred on November 7-9, 2003, when Phi Mu Omega conducted its first Membership Intake Process (MIP). Eight beautiful, savvy, and cultured pearls became members of the chapter. The MIP, held at the Thames Center on the campus of Copiah-Lincoln Community College (Co-Lin), was a highlight of the chapter's short existence. The newly-initiated members and their brief profiles are listed below.

Phi Mu Omega Chapter 2003 MIP/ Members
seated left to right, Rolanda Michelle Bates, Tammy Witherspoon, Sandra Isaac, and Velma Dilworth; standing, Cora Shannon, Tabitha Carr, Madeleine Floyd, and Joyce Tillman

Rolanda Michele Bates
City of Birth: Brookhaven, MS
Parents: Moses and Linda Bates
Sisters/Brothers: Monica, Moses IV, Mark
College(s)/Degree(s): B.S. Univ. of Southern MS.; M.E. Univ. of Phoenix

Tabitha A. Carr
City of Birth: Vicksburg, MS
Parents: Estella and the late George Ashmore

Sisters/Brothers: Emma Markham, Alice Gaulden, Wanda Ashmore, Lois Chess, Janice Berry, Beverly Bates, Floyd, Howard, Samuel, Rodney, and George, Jr.
Child: Regina Carr
College(s)/Degree(s): B.S. Jackson State Univ.; MBA University of Phoenix
Career(s): State Tax Commission Supervisor

Velma Dilworth
City of Birth: Jackson, MS
Parents: The late George and Henrietta Thompson
Sisters/Brothers: Grace Bell, Emma Wilson, George, Jr.
Spouse: Marcus, Sr.
Children: Marcus, Jr., Melvin
College(s)/Degree(s): B.S. and M.S., Jackson State Univ.
Career(s): Teacher/Coach (Retired)

Madeleine Floyd
City of Birth: Liberty, MS
Parents: Milton and Nena Stewart Powell
Sisters/Brothers: George Powell, Booker T. Powell, Milton Powell, Jr., Lanis Powell, Dywane T. Powell
Spouse: Charlie
College(s)/Degree(s): B.S., M. Ed. Southern Univ., Baton Rouge, LA; M.S. Univ. of Southern MS Leadership and Gifted Certification
Career(s): Teacher, Administrator, Adolescent Offender Program (AOP) Counselor (Retired)

Sandra Isaac
City of Birth: Magnolia, MS
Parents: The late Eleas and Ethel P. Addison
Sisters/Brothers: Brenda A. Justice, Jerry Addison, Rickie Addison
Spouse: Mannie, Jr. (deceased)
Children: Corey, Bryce, and Brandon Isaac
College(s)/Degree(s): B.S. Jackson State Univ.; M.S. Alcorn State Univ.
Career(s): Teacher

Awards/Achievements: McComb High School Teacher of the Year (1997/98 and 2004/2005)

Cora Shannon
City of Birth: Hazlehurst, MS
College(s)/Degree(s): B.S. Jackson State Univ.; M.S. Belhaven College, Jackson, MS
Career(s): Banking Administration

Joyce Tillman
City of Birth: Brookhaven, MS
Parents: James and Esther Tillman
Sister: Mary Elizabeth Tillman
College(s)/Degree(s): B.S. Engineering, Mississippi State Univ.
Career(s): Airport Security Administration, Jackson-Evers International

Tammy F. Witherspoon
City of Birth: McComb, MS
Parent: Ruby Felder
Sisters/Brothers: Charlie, Jr., Dorothy Felder, Allie Williams, Vernell Felder, Robert Felder, Nathaniel Garner, Bobby Felder, Teresa Moore, Frank Felder
Spouse: Anthony, I.
Children: Anthony II and Amani Witherspoon
College(s)/Degree(s): B.S. Education Jackson State Univ.; M.S. Special Education, Alcorn State Univ.
Career(s): Mental Health Program Director, Adolescent Opportunity Program Supervisor
Awards/Achievements: First female African-American selectwoman in McComb, MS

The second and larger membership change occurred June 8-10, 2007, when thirteen members completed the MIP process. The new members and their brief profiles are listed below.

Phi Mu Omega Chapter 2007 MIP/Members
members seated left to right, Shirlene Lowery, Juanita Steptoe, Sheila Sartin, Mary Elizabeth Tillman, Mashanda Lee-Thomas, and Janis Anderson; back row Sheanda Davis, Robin Faust, Vanessa Wilbert, Janice Samuels, Ruby Husband, Alfonda Powell, Kayla Freeman.

Janis Anderson
City of Birth: Monticello, MS
Spouse: Jessie Anderson (deceased)
Children: Jessie Vidal Anderson, Kimberly Anderson, Tenitra Hilliard
College(s)/Degree(s): B.S. English Mississippi Valley State Univ.
Career(s): Teacher, Delphi-Packard Technician

Sheanda Bryant Davis
City of Birth: Sumter, SC
Parents: Rev. Dr. Eugene and Alice F. Bryant
Brother: Eugene Bryant, II
Spouse: Earnest R. Davis (deceased)
Child: Zavian M. Davis
College(s)/Degree(s): B.S. Psychology, M.S. Social Work, Jackson State Univ.; Doctor of Theology, AP Clay Theological Seminary, Louisiana
Career(s): Licensed Social Worker and Trainer

Awards/Achievements: Order of Eastern Star Service Award; Family Service Employee of Year

Robin Tyler Faust
City of Birth: Wesson, MS
Parents: Robert and Ruby Tyler
Sisters/Brothers: None
Spouse: George L Faust
Children: Rachel Tyler Faust and Georgette Tyler Faust
College(s)/Degree(s): Associate of Science in Mortuary Science, Northwest MS Comm. Coll., Southaven, MS; B.S. Business Administration, Jackson State Univ.
Career(s): Funeral Director, Embalmer, and Administrator R.E. Tyler Funeral Home, Brookhaven
Awards/Achievements: Graduate International Cemetery, Cremation, Funeral Association (ICCFA) Univ., Univ. of Memphis, Memphis, TN; Certified Funeral Service Practitioner (CFSP); Member Trustmark National Bank Advisory Board; Member Willing Hearts Circle King's Daughters and Sons Medical Center; Member Natchez (MS) chapter of The Links, Inc.; MS Business Journal former "Top 40 Under 40" Business Person in the State of MS

Kayla Dixon Freeman
City of Birth: Brookhaven, MS
Parents: J. Hugh Dixon (deceased) and Alice Ann Dixon
Sisters/Brothers: J. Hugh Dixon, Jr. and Dr. Maronda Elise Dixon
Children: Allison M. Freeman and Mark Nicholas Freeman
College(s)/Degree(s): B.S. Chemistry, Jackson State Univ.; B.S. Pharmacy University of MS, Oxford, MS
Career(s): Pharmacist Walgreens and Wal-Mart, Brookhaven, MS

Ruby M. Husband
City of Birth: Laurel, MS
Parents: Reuben and Wilma McSwain
Sisters/Brothers: Yvonne Powell, Natalie Leverette, Rueben McSwain, Jr.
Spouse: Ray
College(s)/Degree(s): B.S., M.S. University of Southern MS; M.S. Supervision and Administration William Carey Univ.

Career(s): Teacher/Director Special Education in Perry County; Principal, Assistant Superintendent McComb School District
Awards/Achievements: McComb Administrator of the Year, MAE Regional Member of the Year

Mashanda Lee (Thomas)
City of Birth: Flowood, MS
Parents: Dorester Lee and the late Willie David Lee
Sister: Belinda Jackson
Spouse: Ricardo
Child: Bailee Rae Thomas
College(s)/Degree(s): BSW Mississippi College; MSW Jackson State University; University of MS Teach MS Institute Certification
Career(s): Teacher

Shirlene Lowery
City of Birth: Benoit, MS
Parents: Ernest and Eugenia Lowery
Sister: Tabitha L. Williams
Child: Crystal Lowery
College(s)/Degree(s): B.S. Business Administration Mississippi Valley State Univ.
Career(s): Governmental Employee (Vertex Aerospace)

Alfonda Renee Powell Westbrook
City of Birth: McComb, MS
Parents: Alvin and Frances Hogan
Sisters/Brothers: Joseph Lydell Hogan
Spouse: SPC Jonathan Westbrook
Children: Eric Charles Powell II, Jonathan Kaleb Westbrook, and Kirsten Jonee Westbrook
College(s)/Degree(s): B.S. Health Science, M.S. Biology Education, Alcorn State Univ., Lorman, MS
Career(s): Teacher Houston, TX, Southwest Mississippi Community College, Summit, MS, and McComb School District; Case Manager Pike County Department of Human Services, McComb, MS
Awards/Achievements: Member Daughters of the Eastern Stars

Janice Samuels
City of Birth: McComb, MS
Parents: Obydee and Bettye Nunnery
Sisters/Brothers: Thaddaus Nunnery and Juanita Steptoe
Child: Christopher Samuels
College(s)/Degree(s): B.S. Speech Therapy, M.S. Administration and Supervision, Jackson State University
Career(s) Speech Therapist; District Supervisor/Principal North Pike School District, Summit, MS

Sheila Sartin
City of Birth: Brookhaven, MS
Parents: Mack F. and Beatrice M. McCoy
Sisters/Brothers: David McCoy, Maxine Jones, Vicki Kelly, Janice Louis
Spouse: Genoa Sartin III
Children: Trenise Sartin and Genoa Sartin IV
College(s)/Degree(s): B.S. Pharmacy University of MS
Career(s): Pharmacist Money Saver Drugs in Natchez, Southwest Medical Center, McComb, King's Daughters Medical Center, Brookhaven, MS
Awards/Achievements: Trustee, Youth Director Bethel AME Church, Brookhaven, MS; President Ole Brook Gridiron Association

Juanita Steptoe
City of Birth: McComb, MS
Parents: Obydee and Bettye Nunnery
Sisters/Brothers: Janice Samuels and Thaddaus Nunnery
Spouse: Allan Steptoe
Child: Alexia Miaie Steptoe
College(s)/Degree(s): B.S., M.S. Jackson State Univ.; Ed. S. Mississippi College
Career(s): Teacher, Counselor
Awards/Achievements: National Board Certified Counselor and School Counselor

Mary Elizabeth Tillman
City of Birth: Brookhaven, MS
Parents: James and Esther Tillman
Sister: Joyce Tillman
College(s)/Degree(s): B.S. Jackson State University; M.S. Mississippi State University
Career(s): Airport Security Jackson-Evers International

Vanessa F. Wilbert
City of Birth: McComb, MS
Parents: Paul Felder and Gwendolyn Lewis
Sisters/Brothers: Daphne Scott, Damon Felder, Taurean Lewis, Rodrick Lewis
Spouse: Kevin Wilbert
Children: Amante Washington, Jaren Washington, Kevin Wilbert II, Kayla Wilbert, Konner Wilbert
College(s)/Degree(s): B.S. Alcorn State Univ., Lorman, MS; M.S. Leadership Belhaven Univ., Jackson, MS
Career(s): Victim Advocate, Adult Education Instructor, Project Director Victim Assistance Program in Office of Mississippi Attorney General
Awards/Achievements: State Coordinator AKA Day at the Capitol for Mississippi (Rho Lambda Omega, Jackson, MS)

Phi Mu Omega Chapter 2007 MIP
Phi Mu Omega Chapter Members on June 10, 2007
Pictured first row, left to right, charter member Mary Helena Thompson, Celia Pearson, Charter members Doris Jacques, Frances Hogan, Nancy Denham, Lorraine B. Gayden, Nikkitta Beckley-Holloway, and Julia parker; second row, Charter member Marcia Leonard, Sheryl Houston-Jones, Juanita Steptoe, Shirlene Lowery, Joyce Tillman, charter member Esther Tillman, Mary Elizabeth Tillman, Marshanda Lee-Thomas, Madeleine Floyd, Janis Anderson, and Monesa Watts; third row, Tabitha Carr, Robin Faust, Vanessa Wilbert, Claudia Moore, Sheanda Davis, Kendra Armistad, Ruby Husband, charter member Betty Wilson-McSwain, Alfonda Powell, and Kayla Freeman; fourth row, Sheila Sartin, Louise Gombako-Amos, Sandra Isaac, Tammy Witherspoon, Marva Minor Evans, Cora Shannon Maymon, Vonnie Jefferson, Janice Samuels, and charter member Karen Bryant-Luckett.

CHAPTER VIII

FOUNDERS' DAY

2001—Since Phi Mu Omega shares the same birthdate (January 15th) as Alpha Kappa Alpha Sorority, Inc., the chapter considers it a real blessing and honor to celebrate Founders' Day each year. The chapter has held or participated in a Founders' Day celebration every year since its establishment in 2000.

The chapter held its first Founders' Day celebration at 11 a.m. on February 24, 2001, at Southwest Regional Medical Center's Craig Haskins Community Room in McComb—the same room where its chartering luncheon had occurred. Members were so excited to be a chapter that the first celebration was open to the public. *Ivy Leaf* Reporter Leonard sent invitations to approximately 100 individuals. Celebrated as a Founders' Day and Black Heritage Celebration Luncheon, the public luncheon was held at 12 noon with Mrs. Sarah Atkinson Cotton as the guest speaker. Hogan coordinated the "salad festival" menu. Beckley-Holloway and Pearson furnished the punch. Program participants were Bryant-Patterson (mistress of ceremony), Therrell (meditation), Pearson (welcome), Rosalyn Wilkinson of Xi Mu Omega in Columbia, MS (history of Alpha Kappa Alpha), Hogan (history of Phi Mu Omega), Wilson (state of the chapter), Luckett ("Ain't I a Woman"), Beckley-Holloway (introduction of chapter members), Denham (recognition of other Greeks), Bryant-Patterson (praise dance), Leonard (introduction of speaker), and Jacques (acknowledgement of guests).

2002—The Founders' Day celebration held on February 23rd was closed to the public. Coordinated by Denham, it took place in a private dining room at the Western Sizzlin' in Brookhaven at 11 a.m. Participants were Watts (prayer), Jacques (history of Alpha Kappa Alpha), and Denham (history of Phi Mu Omega). President Luckett then conducted the rededication ceremony. The celebration ended with the national hymn and pledge with all chapter members participating.

2003—Founders' Day took place at Bethel AME Church in Brookhaven at 3 p.m. on January 12th. The chapter presented performing arts and a display of Black art.

2004—Founders' Day was a private affair at "The Other Place" in McComb on January 17th. Jacques did the invocation, and Beckley-Holloway and Thompson gave brief histories of the sorority and the chapter respectively. President Gayden gave the State of the Chapter address. Witherspoon led the "Black Family" pledge. A ritual ceremony ended the celebration.

2005—Bethel AME church in Brookhaven was the setting for the celebration on March 19th. Leonard coordinated the closed Founders' Day Celebration, which followed the chapter meeting. Isaac gave the invocation, Wilson and Carr gave brief histories, Gayden made the State of the Chapter presentation, and Jacques recited Maya Angelou's "Still I Rise." The celebration ended with the traditional ritual ceremony.

2006—Chapter members attended the National Founders' Day celebration in January in Jackson, MS.

2007—Members attended the Founders' Day Celebration October 21st at the South Eastern Regional Conference in Nashville, Tennessee, as a precursor to the Centennial National Convention in Washington, D. C. in 2008. Each region of the Sorority celebrated during a different month that year.

2008—February 16th was the date of the Founders' Day Celebration in Brookhaven. President Hogan gave the State of the Chapter address and her daughter Alfonda (a legacy) sang. Other participants on the program were Jacques, Leonard, Beckley-Holloway, and Gayden.

2009-The private celebration followed chapter meeting on March 21st at Bethel AME Church in Brookhaven.

2010—This Founders' Day was special for Phi Mu Omega since it marked ten years of the chapter's timeless service in Southwest Mississippi. Open to the public, it took place at the chartering location on Friday evening, January 15th, at 6 p.m. The first African-American mayor of McComb, MS, Colonel Zachary Patterson (retired), was the special guest. He presented a proclamation to the chapter on the occasion of its 10th anniversary. Pictures from the celebration appeared in the local *Enterprise-Journal* later during the month. For several weeks prior, Guy's Pharmacy on Marion Avenue in McComb used an electronic sign to announce the anniversary. In addition, for the entire month of January the chapter placed a display of paraphernalia at the McComb and Brookhaven public libraries.

McComb Mayor Zach Patterson signs proclamation flanked by Phi Mu Omega chapter members, from left, seated, vice president Marcia Leonard, Doris Jacques and president Nikki Beckley-Holloway; standing, Lorraine Gayden, Janice Samuels, Celia Pearson, Madeleine Floyd, Sandra Isaac, Juanita Steptoe, Ruby Husband, Tammy Witherspoon, Alfonda Powell, Sheila Sartin, Frances Hogan, Robin Faust, Karen Bryant-Luckett, Kayla Freeman, Barbara Scott and Nancy Denham.

2011—Founders' Day was celebrated following chapter meeting at Bethel AME Church in Brookhaven on March 19th. At Standards

Chairman Gayden's request, members read the Code of Ethics during the ceremony and signed it following the ceremony.

2012—Phi Mu Omega participated in a joint celebration, "Celebrating the Legacy of Sisterhood through Timeless Service," with graduate chapters Beta Delta Omega, Rho Lambda Omega, Upsilon Upsilon Omega, Mu Xi Omega, Zeta Delta Omega, Omicron Beta Omega and undergraduate chapters Gamma Omicron (Tougaloo College), Gamma Rho (Jackson State), and Gamma Phi (Alcorn State) at Woodworth Chapel on the campus of Tougaloo on February 19th at 3 p.m. Soror Glenda Glover of Beta Delta Omega conceived the plan and invited other central and southwest MS chapters to participate. International Vice President Dorothy Buckhanan Wilson was the guest speaker. Tougaloo's President, sorority member Beverly Hogan, hosted a lovely reception in the President's home following the celebration. Phi Mu Omega members Karen Bryant Luckett, Marcia Leonard, Doris Jacques, Lorraine B. Gayden, and Nikkitta Beckley-Holloway attended the celebration.

2013—Founders' Day followed the chapter meeting on February 16th in the McComb public library conference room. Several members went to lunch at Applebee's for sisterly fellowship following the ceremony. Soror Robin Reed, a visiting general member due to her husband's uncertain military assignments, was present and participated.

2012 Joint Founders' Day at Tougaloo College: seated from left to right, Karen Bryant-Luckett, Doris Jacques, Marcia Leonard, International Vice President Dorothy Buckhanan Wilson, Lorraine Gayden, and Nikkitta Beckley-Holloway.

Phi Mu Omega Founders' Day February 2013 seated left to right, Ruby Husband, Doris Jacques and Marcia Leonard; standing left to right, Paquita McCray, Karen Bryant-Luckett, Barbara Scott, Lorraine Gayden, Claudia Moore, Tammy Witherspoon, Sandra Isaac, Katrina Sartin and Mary Helena Thompson.

Chapter IX

CHAPTER PROGRAMS (2000-2014)

ON TRACK (2000-2002)

When Phi Mu Omega was chartered in 2000, Soror Norma Solomon White became the 25th International President and the first legacy member to hold that position. White's theme during her administration was "Blazing New Trails" with a focus on Family, Economics, Education, Health, and the Arts. Her thematic symbol showed an elegant woman in a pink dress holding a torch in her raised right hand. The five foci were listed vertically and were undergirded by the phrase "Leadership Development." White also began the PIMS (Partnership in Math and Science) program and launched the ON TRACK program (Organizing, Nurturing, Teambuilding, Respecting, Achieving, Counseling, and Knowing) for after-school programs targeting at-risk elementary school students. Her legacies to Alpha Kappa Alpha include building 10 schools in post-apartheid South Africa, establishing funding partnerships with the US Department of Health to promote women's health, and initiating National Founders' Day observances.

Phi Mu Omega got right on track with its Alpha Beau reception (family), census 2000 and prom 2000 (economic empowerment), annual scholarship ball (education), Relay for Life team in Brookhaven in May (health), and plans for the Black Heritage Celebration of African art in February 2001 (arts). From the annual Scholarship Ball (education) profit of $1,287.11, the chapter awarded scholarships of $250 each to Melissa Hockett of Franklin County High School and Stephanie Woodard of McComb High School, with the remaining amount of $787.11 to be spent on other community service projects. The signature "Holiday Blood Drive" at Wal-Mart in December netted 25 pints of blood. The chapter provided refreshments and "jingle bells" for donors.

Activities for 2001 included participation in Alpha Phi Alpha's Martin Luther King Day celebration on January 15th in Brookhaven, a Black Heritage Celebration Luncheon on February 24th following the Founders' Day observance and Prom 2001 held at Alexander Junior High School on March 3rd, where participants were awarded cash prizes. The prom was coordinated by Soror Margaret Stribling who owned a dress shop in Brookhaven. In March another family project was conducting an Ivy Beyond the Wall ceremony for Soror Lillie Turner and providing a meal for her family. Sorors Wilson, Luckett, and Denham also attended the South Eastern Regional Conference in Tunica, MS, in March. Soror Luckett chaired the team for the Relay for Life in Brookhaven on May 4-5th which raised $1100. Soror Beckley-Holloway implemented an "on track" after-school program for fifth graders at the Boys and Girls Club of Brookhaven and served ice cream to 100 children in June. Soror Hogan chaired AKA Coat Day on Oct. 27th in conjunction with "Make a Difference Day" by collecting and cleaning coats for Soror Taylor to distribute to needy students at Alexander Junior High School in Brookhaven. Sorors Beckley-Holloway, Denham, Parker, and Watts served as hostesses for the Brookhaven Little Theater's production of "The Curious Savage" and "Catfish Moon" on November 16th. Sorors provided flyers with resource and contact information at McComb High School's college night on Sept. 17th and Hazlehurst High's on November 7th. Soror Luckett chaired the signature "Holiday Blood Drive" at Wal-Mart in McComb on December 8th which netted 22 pints. The chapter donated excess refreshments from the blood drive to the Boys and Girls Club of Southwest Mississippi in McComb. Finally, the chapter held its 2001 Scholarship Ball fundraiser on December 8th at the Lincoln County Multipurpose Building in Brookhaven.

For 2002, Phi Mu Omega hosted a table at the reception following Alpha Phi Alpha's Martin Luther King Day celebration at Alexander Junior High School in Brookhaven, for which the chapter received a certificate of appreciation. The chapter held a Leadership Conference for high school students at McComb High School from 10 a.m.-12 noon on February 6th. Jets of Brookhaven and African-American-owned Thomas Fashions for Men of McComb hosted "Prom 2002" at the McComb High School Auditorium on February 7th. Sorors

Gayden, Leonard, and Wilson served as hostesses. Sorors Denham, Luckett, Hogan, and Wilson attended the 71st Regional Conference that was held on March 7-10th in Huntsville, AL, and participated in the welcome activities with Cluster IV for the South Eastern Regional Conference to be held in Jackson, MS, on March 27-30, 2003. The chapter participated in Relay for Life in Brookhaven again on May 3-4th in 2002 in memory of Turner and in honor of survivor and chapter member Beckley-Holloway. Chapter members Gayden (a Habitat board member), Jacques, Luckett, Chilibra Patterson, Pearson, Taylor, and Thompson prepared and served lunch to Pike County Habitat for Humanity volunteers in McComb on May 11, 2002.

At the 2002 Boule in Orlando, FL, Soror Linda Marie White became the 26th Supreme Basileus of Alpha Kappa Alpha Sorority, Inc. The theme for her administration was **"The Spirit of AKA"** with a focus on after-school tutorial programs for K-3rd grade students in an Ivy Reading AKAdemy. Her programs centered on the Black family. Soror White launched the Young Authors' Program which led to the publication of two volumes of *The Spirit Within: Voices of Young Authors* anthologies and secured a $1.5 million US Department of Education grant. She also promoted volunteerism; provided more than $20 million in financial support to disadvantaged youth, the elderly, and Black families; donated time and money to hurricane disaster relief efforts following Hurricanes Katrina, Rita, and Wilma; and launched the Sorority's first international web site.

Phi Mu Omega completed its ON TRACK agenda for the remainder of 2002 and began to implement programs for "The Spirit of AKA." The chapter partnered with the Salvation Army for Coat Day in October to address White's plan to help Black families. Soror Parker disseminated Breast Cancer Awareness flyers at Bethel AME Church in Brookhaven, and sorors wore pink ribbons. The annual "Holiday Blood Drive" was November 16th that year to coincide with Sickle Cell Awareness, resulting in fifteen pints of blood being collected. The final activity was the signature Scholarship Ball dinner-dance on December 14th at the Lincoln County Multipurpose Building. The three latter projects also supported "The Spirit of AKA" initiative of providing assistance to Black families.

"The Spirit of AKA" (2002-2006)

Phi Mu Omega Programs(2002-2006)

After Linda Marie White's installation as the 26th international president of Alpha Kappa Alpha at the Orlando convention in July 2002, the "Spirit" campaign began in earnest. White continued Norma Solomon's White's trailblazing spirit as she launched the Sorority's first international website. Her "Spirit of AKA" theme not only launched initiatives focused on the Black family but also highlighted programs that focused on the youth. The signature program of her administration, the Young Authors' Program under the leadership of International Program Committee chairman Juanita Sims Doty of Beta Delta Omega chapter in Jackson, MS, resulted in the publication of two volumes of *The Spirit Within: Voices of Young Authors, an* anthology of stories written by youth from grades 2 to 6. The daughter of soror Deborah Gambrell Chambers of Theta Sigma Omega chapter in Hattiesburg, MS, brought great pride to Mississippi as an "author" from the South Eastern region. Phi Mu Omega had submitted entries for the contest, but none had been selected. The chapter applauded South Eastern's young author and claimed her with pride since Hattiesburg is only 70 miles east of McComb. In addition, soror Chambers had relatives living and working in McComb. *The Spirit Within . . . . .was the highlight at the 2004* Boule held at the Opryland Hotel in Nashville, TN, where the nation's first lady Laura Bush commended the "authors" and addressed convention delegates at a plenary session. Security was extremely tight during Mrs. Bush's visit as expected. Volume II of *The Spirit Within . . . appeared in print in 2006.*

During the "Spirit" administration, White led the charge in promoting volunteerism, and Phi Mu Omega followed her lead. Notable during this period was the $20 million in financial donations that Alpha Kappa Alpha Sorority, Inc. made to support disadvantaged youth, the elderly, Black families and "AKAdemies" as well as schools built in Africa under her leadership. Unfortunately, White died at age 68 in Chicago on February 26, 2010, after a lengthy illness.

Karen Luckett (2002-2003) and Lorraine Gayden (2004-2005) shared chapter leadership during the "spirit" years. Karen was a scientist, humanitarian, and a dentist by trade. Karen, as with a surgeon's hands, handled members with a soft but effective touch in order to get the desired results. The first membership intake process occurred November 7-9, 2003, at the Thames Center on the campus of Copiah-Lincoln Community College to enlarge chapter membership. Inductees were Rolanda Michele Bates, Tabitha Carr, and Joyce Tillman of Brookhaven; Velma Dilworth of Jackson, MS; Madeleine Floyd of Centreville in Wilkinson County; Sandra Isaac and Tammy Witherspoon of McComb; and Cora Shannon of Hazlehurst.

Officers who served with Karen were vice president Lorraine Gayden, secretary Frances Hogan, assistant secretary Marcia Leonard, financial secretary Margaret Therrell, corresponding secretary Nikki Holloway, treasurer Celia Pearson, hostess Mary Helena Thompson, *Ivy Leaf* reporter Julia Parker, doorkeeper Zelphia Taylor, historian Nancy Denham, and chaplain Monesa Watts (see member roster in appendix for chapter membership between 2002 and 2006).

Phi Mu Omega continued its signature health initiative by supporting the American Cancer Society's Relay for Life program in Brookhaven in 2002—this time in honor of chapter member Nikki Holloway and its annual Holiday Blood Drive in December. To focus on the Black family, the chapter awarded scholarships (see appendix for scholarships recipients for 2002 and 2003).

By contrast, Gayden—a humanities scholar, social worker, and teacher–was passionate and goal-oriented and used fervent orations to accomplish desired results. Notwithstanding their different leadership styles, both Luckett and Gayden were able to lead the chapter forward during the "Spirit" years.

Officers for 2004-2005 were Vice President Frances Hogan, secretary Monesa Watts, assistant secretary Betty Wilson, financial secretary Celia Pearson, corresponding secretary Mary Helena Thompson, treasurer Margaret Therrell, hostess Nancy Denham, doorkeeper Julia Parker, chaplain Doris Jacques, historian Marcia Leonard, *Ivy Leaf* reporter Nikki Holloway, and parliamentarian Karen Luckett (see member roster in appendix for chapter membership in 2004 and 2005).

Phi Mu Omega participated in other "Spirit" programs proffered by White, who realized that many traditional public schools were not performing at highly successful levels or adequately preparing students for the 21st century age of global competition and educational preparedness. The Ivy AKAdemy initiative, which focused on after-school tutorial programs for kindergarten through third grade students, motivated Phi Mu Omega to begin tutorial programs at local schools and at local Boys and Girls Clubs in Southwest Mississippi. The chapter also held a financial literacy workshop for high school students at Copiah-Lincoln Community College on March 5, 2005. These workshops were conducted by chapter members Marcia Leonard and Nikkitta Beckley-Holloway. White successfully sought and received over $1.5 million in grants from the U.S. Department of Education. This was a remarkable achievement since President George W. Bush had reorganized the federal Elementary and Secondary Act (ESEA) of 1965 as the "No Child Left Behind Act" (NCLB), which he signed into law on January 8, 2002, as Public Law 107-110. Since Phi Mu Omega neither had applied for nor had received any grant funding, its local programs were limited but were implemented using available chapter funds derived from fundraising projects. The chapter's primary education focus continued to be providing scholarships for graduating young ladies to allow them to further their post-secondary education with funds raised at the annual Scholarship Ball held in December of each year. It was the chapter's hope and desire that these young ladies would have an opportunity to become fellow members of this great sisterhood. Fortunately, several of the recipients are now members of this prestigious sorority (see appendix for scholarship recipients in 2004 and 2005).

Following the devastation left by Hurricane Katrina, which literally destroyed much of the New Orleans area inhabited by Blacks and much of the Gulf Coast on August 29, 2005, Phi Mu Omega purchased school uniforms for children who had migrated into Southwest Mississippi following Katrina and were attending Amite County schools in Liberty, MS. Sorority members from across the United

States and abroad supplied much-needed time and money for hurricane relief efforts. Later, during the first year of President Barbara Ann McKinzie's administration, the biannual Leadership Seminar in July 2007 was relocated from its originally proposed site in Montreal, Quebec, Canada, to New Orleans in order to pump money into the economy of that great cosmopolitan city. The Seminar did not get to Montreal until July 2013. During the 2007 Seminar in New Orleans, Alpha Kappa Alpha built a Habitat for Humanity house in New Orleans as well as a Habitat house on the Mississippi Gulf Coast. The Willis family on the Gulf Coast was extremely grateful. The Sorority continued to make contributions to the Willis family for several years following the dedication of the home. Phi Mu Omega had partnered with the Pike County (MS) Habitat affiliate in McComb earlier in 2002 to provide lunch for volunteers working on a house on the corner of Bendat and Seminary Streets by providing lunch and fellowshipping with the volunteers. Chapter members and volunteers enjoyed the Popeye's fried chicken and the homemade side dishes. Gayden has been a Habitat board member for twenty (20) years. She has served on its selection and nurturing committees, as publicity chairman, and is secretary for the current board.

In 2005, the chapter began its Martin Luther King Day of Service program by requesting members to visit the elderly in nursing homes or deliver meals to sick and shut-ins in various communities. At schools, the "Kaps for Kids" program was initiated to provide woolen caps for students who needed them during the winter months. The chapter donated $1150 to the Relay for Life campaign in Brookhaven and manned a booth which sold pink and green refreshment items— pink lemonade and pickles. During the summer, the chapter hosted a cookout for fifty high school students in the Upward Bound program at Copiah-Lincoln Community College on the recommendation of program director and chapter member Julia Parker. The chapter also held its retreat at the Magnolia Terrace, a Black-owned bed and breakfast in Magnolia, MS. In memory of charter member Lillie Turner and in honor of charter member Nikki Beckley-Holloway, the chapter observed one of its signature programs--Breast Cancer Awareness—in October. For this observation in 2005, members purchased, widely distributed, and wore symbolic pink ribbon pins.

The chapter's annual Veterans' Day program has occured every year on November 11th. In 2005, the program took place at McComb Extended Care on Locust Street in McComb. Chairmen Doris Jacques and Madeleine Floyd prepared care packages and presented certificates to resident veterans. Other members participated on the program which consisted of prayer, patriotic songs, remarks from retired veteran VFW Post Commander and McComb selectman Melvin Joe Johnson, and information from Ladies' Auxiliary President Mildred Hall. The chapter saluted active duty National Guardsman and Phi Mu Omega member Tabitha Carr, who attended the program in uniform, and celebrated her safe return from her recent tour of duty in Japan. The chapter got into the holiday spirit by participating in Christmas parades in McComb and Brookhaven. The annual Scholarship Ball dinner-dance fundraiser was held at the Lincoln County Multipurpose Building with more than 300 guests in attendance and live entertainment by "24/7" of Jackson. The 2005 Ball proved to be a good year for fundraising which allowed the chapter to award $4500 in scholarships in 2006.

Other chapter programs and activities during the "spirit" years were a Black Family Picnic at Percy Quin State Park and contributions to the Pike County Coalition for its Black History Bowl, the Pike county branch of the NAACP, the Boys and Girls Club of Southwest Mississippi, the Educational Advancement Foundation, and to a foreign mission in Africa.

Phi Mu Omega members at 2004 Scholarship Ball; pictured are, at bottom left of staircase, from left, Nikki Beckley-Holloway, Joyce t. Tillman, Madeleine P. Floyd, Velma C. Dilworth and Celia g. Pearson. From top left of staircase going down, Tabitha A. Carr, Monesa Watts, Betty Spann Wilson, Sharrieffah Z.M. Sharieff, Dr. Karen Bryant Luckett, Lorraine B. Gayden, Sandra A. Issac, Tammy F. Witherspoon, and Cora Q. Shannon. From top right staircase, Frances B. Hogan, Mary Helena R. Thompson, Nancy W. Denham, Margaret W. Therrell, Michele Bates, Julia Wright Parker, Doris Jacques and Marcia S. Leonard.

The "ESP" Years of Alpha Kappa Alpha (2006-2010)

PHI MU OMEGA CHAPTER PROGRAMS (2006-2010)

The year 2006 brought about new local and international leadership. Phi Mu Omega's newly installed officers for 2006 were president Frances Hogan, vice president Nikki Beckley-Holloway, secretary Betty Wilson (now McSwain), assistant secretary Joyce Tillman, financial secretary Nancy Denham, Treasurer Tabitha Carr, corresponding secretary Madeleine Floyd, hostess Karen Bryant Luckett, doorkeeper Mary Helena Thompson, historian Doris Jacques, chaplain Velma Dilworth, parliamentarian Julia Parker, and *Ivy Leaf* reporter Lorraine B. Gayden (see member roster in appendix for chapter membership between 2006 and 2010). Gayden, Hogan, and Denham represented the chapter at the South Eastern regional conference in Memphis in March where Denham became a golden member.

The sorority installed Barbara A. McKinzie as the 27th international president at the biannual international meeting in Detroit, MI, in July 2006. Phi Mu Omega's attendees were Hogan, Floyd, Gayden, and "honey do" Robert Gayden. The delegation stayed across the border in Windsor, Ontario, Canada with numerous other members from across the country. That was an interesting experience because each time a bus load of members crossed the border, each passenger had to disembark, submit a passport for review, go through customs and border patrol, and climb onto the bus again for the trip to the convention center or to the hotels! McKinzie's administration ushered in "The Heart of ESP: An Extraordinary Service Program". The acronym also connoted "Economics, Sisterhood, and Partnerships"; "Extra Special Programs"; "Economics, Service, and Partnerships"; and "Every Soror Participates". "ESP" programs included the non-traditional entrepreneur, the economic keys to success related to economic literacy, economic growth for the black family with an emphasis on black males, an undergraduate initiative, and health resources management.

Phi Mu Omega Program chairman Beckley-Holloway and the chapter members got started right away on the economics agenda. For the nontraditional entrepreneur, the chapter initiated a signature program—"Jazz by the Lake"—to showcase the talents of nontraditional entrepreneurs including caterers, a jazz band, and visual artists. Auctioneer Warren Banks conducted a live auction during the event at the Percy Quin State Park Convention Center in McComb in 2006. The chapter also held a reception at the Martin Luther King Center in McComb for newly-elected Mississippi State Representative and Amite County native Angela Cockerham, Esquire, and Valerie Jones Turner, DDS, a Pike county native who had recently opened Mississippi Dentistry for Children. The chapter donated children's books for Dr. Turner's office and a set of Black History books to the McComb Public Library. Both Cockerham and Turner later reactivated with Phi Mu Omega. The chapter also donated to the Brookhaven Little Theater and members served as hostesses during a production.

Economic literacy programs included a financial literacy workshop at the McComb High School Business and Technology Complex where chapter members Wilson-McSwain and Hogan were director and teacher respectively. Mitzi Dease Paige, Esquire, of Beta Delta Omega chapter in Jackson, MS, conducted the workshop. Chapter members Kendra Armistad and Vonnie Jefferson organized and operated the Earn, Save, and Prosper (ESP) Kids Club at Wesson Attendance Center in 2007.

To promote the economic growth of the black family, the chapter donated prize money for the Pike County Coalition's annual Black History Bowl and to the Pike Branch of the NAACP. The annual Scholarship Ball dinner-dance fundraiser at the Lincoln County Multipurpose Building in 2006 allowed the chapter to award $4000 in scholarships in 2007 (see appendix for recipients).

Under the economic growth of the family initiative, the chapter held a Father-Son brunch at the Day's Inn of McComb in 2006. On the Saturday before Father's Day, the chapter held the event for several years thereafter with guest speakers Alvin Hogan, Minister John Johnson, Elder Gregory Partman, Robert Lamkin, and Kelvin Wilbert of the Fatherhood Initiative. The chapter also supported the McComb High School Cultural Diversity Awareness Club for male vocational students at the Business and Technology Complex, held a leadership luncheon, hosted a Student Leadership Conference at the Thames Center on the campus of Copiah-Lincoln Community College on September 23, 2006, for junior high and high school students residing in Southwest Mississippi, and held its annual Veterans' Day program atCountry Brook Nursing Home in Brookhaven. Co-chairmen Jacques and Floyd prepared personal care packages and certificates for resident veterans.

An exciting event occurred for the chapter in 2007—thirteen new members joined the chapter during a second Membership Intake Process! Initiates were Janis Anderson and Sheanda Davis of Monticello; Juanita Steptoe, Ruby Husband, Alfonda Hogan Powell Westbrook (a legacy), and Vanessa Wilbert of McComb; Janice Samuels of Summit; Robin Faust, Kayla Freeman, Sheila Sartin, and Elizabeth Tillman of Brookhaven; and Shirlene Lowery and Mashanda Lee of Canton (See Significant Membership Changes for profiles).

To implement the health resources platform, the chapter delivered meals to elderly shut-ins, visited nursing home residents, or took a loved one to a medical appointment in observance of the Martin Luther King Day of Service. The Kaps for Kids program provided woolen caps and gloves for needy students in Brookhaven elementary schools and at McComb High School. A Cardiovascular Health Day was held in February. Phi Mu Omega also partnered with members of Delta Sigma Theta and Zeta Phi Beta to host a wellness brunch at the Percy Quin State Park convention center on March 24, 2007, with Dr. Sharon Collins and registered nurse Cindy Johns as presenters. As always, the chapter participated in one of its signature programs, the American Cancer Society's Relay for Life. The chapter's 2006 team had raised $2948.60 for the relay held in McComb on May 12th. For 2007, the chapter donated $500 each to the Wilkinson County and the Lawrence County relays. For Sickle Cell Awareness in September of 2006, the chapter held a walk at the track at Southwest Mississippi Regional Medical Center and in 2007 donated $350 to the Mississippi Sickle Cell chapter in honor of member Tammy Witherspoon's son

Anthony II. Tammy and her husband Anthony had another son Armani who was able to donate good cells to cure his brother. The chapter always commemorated Breast Cancer Awareness month in October in memory of deceased charter member Lillie Turner and in honor of chapter members who are breast cancer survivors. On October 20, 2007, the chapter held a breast cancer awareness program at Walker's Chapel Free Will Baptist Church with Mississippi Cancer Institute director Dr. Burnett Hanson as the featured speaker. Personalized chapter pens and symbolic pink-ribbon pins were distributed. The chapter's signature "Holiday Blood Drive" was held December 4, 2006, and December 1, 2007, at the Wal-Mart in McComb.

Internally, the chapter held its leadership development retreat on August 18, 2006, at Broma's Deli in Brookhaven. A number of Phi Mu Omega members attended the December 2006 cluster workshop and meeting at the Marriott in downtown Jackson. The highlight of the meeting was a salute to ailing 14th South Eastern regional director Ernestine Holloway. Phi Mu Omega was among the chapters that presented a gift to Holloway for her leadership as Graduate Advisor of Gamma Omicron at Tougaloo for many years and as regional director. The chapter's 2007 retreat was held in August at the Black, family-owned Lake Lu Varn Resort in Magnolia.

Since 2007 was the year leading up to the Centennial celebration for Alpha Kappa Alpha, McComb's first African-American mayor, Colonel Zachary Patterson (retired), issued a proclamation to the chapter on October 30, 2007, and the mayor and city councilmen of Brookhaven issued a proclamation on November 7, 2007. The South Eastern region held its 2007 regional conference on October 18-21st of that year in Nashville, TN. Ten chapter members attended that regional!

An unprecedented event occurred in the chapter's November 2007 election—the chapter chose to re-elect a sitting president for another two-year term. Although chapter bylaws permit a second term for officers, a reelection had never occurred before. Frances Hogan would serve as president for 2008 and 2009 along with most of the officers from her first term. Marcia Leonard replaced Wilson as secretary in March 2008. The chapter also reclaimed Barbara Scott in early 2008.

Nationally, the country was in a deep recession and the Bush era was coming to an end. Little did anyone expect to witness the election of the first African-American President of the United States of America. Barack Hussein Obama was elected President in November 2008!

Chapter activities is 2008 for the nontraditional entrepreneur were a "Move on it, Act on it Seminar" at Co-Lin Community College and "Jazz by the Lake" at Percy Quin State Park in McComb. The ESP Kids Club at Hazlehurst Middle School taught "AKA-nomics." To support the Black family, the chapter participated in the Martin Luther King Day program on January 20th at Alexander Junior High School in Brookhaven, awarded scholarships in May, held an "Etiquette, Self-Esteem, and Prevention" (ESP) workshop, hosted a Student Leadership Conference on the campus of Southwest MS Community College (SMCC) just northeast of McComb on September 6th, and held its first Calendar Girl Cotillion at SMCC on November 8th. The chapter held Veterans' Day programs in both McComb and Brookhaven on the 11th of November. Mississippi State Representative David W. Myers and retired veteran Melvin Johnson attended the program in McComb. The biggest economic empowerment initiative, the signature Scholarship dinner-dance in December, was held at the McComb Event Center in 2008.

Health resources management activities included a "day of pampering" for members. The chapter netted $2700 for the Relay for Life on May 2nd in Brookhaven. The signature "Kaps for Kids" program provided wool caps and small heaters for children and their families. The chapter sponsored a National Women's Health Week program at the walking track in Brookhaven on May 10th, hosted a sickle cell awareness walk at Southwest Mississippi Regional Medical Center walking track in McComb on September 27th , and co-hosted a wellness brunch with members of Delta Sigma Theta and Zeta Phi Beta at Southwest Mississippi Community College on October 11, 2008, with Dr. Sandra Underwood of the University of Wisconsin-Milwaukee as the speaker. TV personality Maggie Wade of Jackson served as the emcee. Breast cancer awareness programs have always been a priority in October. The holiday blood drive was held at the McComb Wal-Mart on November 29th.

The annual retreat was held at the Hampton Inn and Suites on August 15th and at the Pike County Bank Community Room on August 16th. Along with chapter program plans for 2009, the chapter also made intermal leadership development a priority for 2009.

The chapter got off to a dashing start in 2009 and kept busy by hosting an economic empowerment summit with ESP Kids' workshops on January 19th. To support the black family initiative, the chapter operated a male book club for 5-8 graders during the week of February 23-28th and hosted a Father-Son brunch on June 20th with McComb High School band director Robert Lamkin as the speaker. On April 4th, "Jazz by the Lake" was in full swing at the Percy Quin Convention Center. The chapter also fielded a Relay for Life team for May 8th in McComb, participated in the Sorority-wide National Women's Health Initiative on May 15th, and awarded scholarships in May. The chapter kept very busy right up until the summer break! Gayden represented the chapter at the Leadership Seminar in Anchorage, AK, from July 15-18th. On August 14, 2009, the chapter resumed its planning during the retreat at the Thames Center at Co-Lin after a brief summer break. The chapter planned several activities, including a second "Calendar Girl" cotillion, a sickle cell awareness program on September 27th, a breast cancer awareness and Student Leadership Conference at Co-Lin on October 17th, the Veterans' Day program on November 11th, the holiday blood drive on December 12th, and the scholarship ball at the National Guard Armory in Brookhaven on December 19th where "BRW" from New Orleans provided live entertainment. Much to the delight of ABE/GED Program Director Alvin Hogan, in 2009 the chapter awarded a $1000 scholarship to non-traditional student Ebony Patterson who enrolled at Alcorn State University that fall.

Martin Luther King celebration at Alexander Junior High
School in Brookhaven. Pictured are Kayla Freeman, Vonnie
Jefferson, Nancy Denham, Nikkitta Beckley-Holloway,
Francis Hogan, Sheila Sartin and Lorraine Gayden.

Phi Mu Omega's Sickle Cell Walk at Southwest MS Regional
Medical Center's walking track (September, 2007); pictured
first row, Sheanda Davis, Barbara Scott, Tammy Witherspoon,
Alfonda Powell, Vanessa Wilbert, and Frances Hogan; top row
Sheila Sartin, Marcia Leonard, Doris Jacques, Sandra Isaac,
Janice Samuels, Angela Samuels, and Karen Bryant-Luckett.

Blood Drive at Wal-Mart, from left to right, Barbara Scott,
Sandra Isaac, Shirlene Lowery, Madeleine Floyd, Karen Bryant-
Luckett, Mary Helena Thompson and Vanessa Wilbert.

PHI MU OMEGA PROGRAMS (2010-2014)

Global Leadership Through Timeless Service

The chapter began 2010 with new president Nikki Beckley-Holloway at the helm. Officers who served with Beckley-Holloway were vice president Marcia Leonard, secretary Tammy Witherspoon, assistant secretary Ruby Husband, financial secretary Claudia Moore, corresponding secretary Karen Bryant Luckett, treasurer Margaret Therrell, hostess Vanessa Wilbert, doorkeeper Mary Helena Thompson, *Ivy Leaf* reporter Madeleine Floyd, historian Lorraine B. Gayden, custodian Frances Hogan, chaplain Sheanda Davis, Th. D., and parliamentarian Julia Parker. Although membership experienced a slight decrease, the chapter was very much alive and well (see member roster in appendix).

Phi Mu Omega celebrated ten (10) years of sisterhood and service to Southwest Mississippi in 2010. The month-long celebration consisted of displays of Alpha Kappa Alpha and Phi Mu Omega memorabilia at the McComb and the Brookhaven public libraries. The chapter held its anniversary and Founders' Day celebration on Friday, January 15th in the C.O. Haskins Community Room at Southwest Mississippi Regional Medical Center—the same room where the chartering luncheon had taken place. The health-related theme was "A New Year, A New You." Retired Army Colonel and the first African-American mayor of the City of McComb, the Honorable Zachary Patterson, presented a proclamation to the chapter at the celebration.

The first part of 2010 was devoted to ESP health resources management programs, including the annual blood drive on January 16th at the Wal-Mart in McComb. The chapter saluted members Sheila Sartin and Kayla Freeman during Black History month as the first two African-American registered pharmacists in Brookhaven and participated in the Relay for Life in Brookhaven on April 20 with the theme "A Cure for Cancer—Not an Impossible Dream." Chapter member and survivor Sheila Sartin was a featured speaker. The chapter contributed $1763 to the American Cancer Society.

Program chairman Leonard got right to work on the "Global Leadership Through Timeless Service" initiatives with a health initiative. The annual blood drive, normally held in December, took place at the Wal-Mart in McComb on January 16th following chapter meeting. Other health initiatives followed throughout the year. On October 23rd, Shelia Sartin chaired the chapter's Breast Cancer Awareness event at center court of the Edgewood Mall in McComb from 10 a.m. to 2 p.m. with the theme "Early Detection is the Best Protection." Chapter members wore "Fight Cancer Like a Girl" or other breast cancer awareness T-shirts. The event included prize giveaways such as theme bags, breast self-examination shower door hangers, bookmarks, stickers, balloons, and information packets. Medical consultations and presentations, as well as an information board, were also available to the public. The event truly made an impact on visitors to the mall that day! The signature holiday blood drive took place on December 3rd at the McComb Wal-Mart.

At the international meeting in St. Louis in July 2010, the sisterhood witnessed a leadership change as Carolyn House Stewart, Esquire, became the first attorney and the first international president to serve a full term in the sorority's second century. St. Louis was alive with anticipation as attendees received the "Global Leadership Through Timeless Service" initiatives for 2010-2014. Stewart's programs would include the signature Emerging Young Leaders (EYL) program; the global poverty, health, economic security, social justice and human rights programs; and the internal leadership for external service mandate.

Economic security and social justice and human rights issues projects implemented by the chapter included participation in the Martin Luther King Day of Service on January 18th by visiting elderly and disabled individuals and delivering meals. Beckley-Holloway, Nancy Denham, and Gayden attended the Brookhaven Greek Unity Luncheon that day at the Country Fisherman in Brookhaven. In 2010, chapter member

Dr. Valerie Turner and her husband Terrance had opened a Greek and fraternal store in downtown Summit, MS, called "Peaches and Pearls."

In the area of social justice and human rights, Gayden unsuccessfully ran for a seat on the McComb School District board of trustees, but Witherspoon won a seat on the McComb City board of selectmen representing ward 3 and became one of the first African-American females on the board. Chapter members assisted with both campaigns and attended the victory celebration and swearing-in ceremony for Witherspoon. In October of that year, the McComb School District inducted Dr. Turner into the McComb High School Hall of Fame. Phi Mu Omega members were on a roll!

Social justice and human rights and economic security issues continued to be paramount to the chapter as indicated by contributions to the Pike County Coalition's Black History Bowl competition among high school students for cash prizes, the awarding of $4000 in scholarships (see appendix), and the continuation of the Father-Son brunch at the Days Inn of McComb on June 19th. Co-sponsors of the brunch were St. Catherine Spiritual Church (Hogan's Church), 24th Street Church of Christ, Walker's Chapel Free Will Baptist Church (Gayden's church), and the Boys and Girls Club of Southwest Mississippi. Kelvin Wilbert, a counselor with the Fatherhood Initiative of Jackson, MS, and the husband of chapter member Vanessa, was the guest speaker. The Summit Learning Literacy Council, directed by Hogan's husband Alvin, provided a plaque for the speaker. The Walker's Chapel Mime Team provided entertainment. The second biannual Calendar Girl Cotillion, "Elegance in Bloom," took place on September 4th with five participants. Kreshasha Torrence (now an AKA) became "Miss Calendar Girl," and the project was a successful fundraiser to support the chapter's programs. The chapter's signature Veterans' Day program took place at Country Brook Manor nursing home in Brookhaven, where the chapter donated funds to purchase games for veteran residents and presented certificates and medals to the resident veterans. Members also participated in several "reading rallies" sponsored by the McComb School District by marching in parades and reading to preschool and elementary students. As usual, members rang bells for the Salvation Army at Wal-Mart and McComb

Market on several days. At the chapter's invitation, several inactive members also participated in the bell ringing. The chapter made a financial contribution to the Lincoln County Boys and Girls Club and held its signature fund raising Scholarship Ball at the Lincoln County Multipurpose Building on December 11th with entertainment by the "Essence of Soul."

On December 4th, the chapter entered a float entitled "A Rocking Christmas" in the McComb Christmas parade. Cotillion participants rode the float.

Internal Leadership Training was addressed in monthly meetings and during the retreat at Co-Lin on August 2-3, 2010. Topics had been pre-selected by the standards committee and approved by the chapter.

Unfortunately, hostess Vanessa Wilbert transferred to Rho Lambda Omega in Jackson at the end of 2010 to be closer to her job and parliamentarian Julia Parker resigned. Mary Helena Thompson replaced Wilbert and Betty Wilson-McSwain was appointed parliamentarian in February 2011. The chapter also experienced the loss of five other members for various reasons, leaving the chapter with twenty-five (25) members. Even though the losses impacted the chapter, spirits remained high and the timeless service of the chapter was not diminished (see member roster in appendix). The chapter also adopted its first Standard Operating Procedures (SOP) at its February 19, 2011, meeting.

In 2011, several members attended the annual NAACP Youth Council breakfast at Southwest Mississippi Regional Medical Center, delivered meals to elderly and shut-ins, and attended the Martin Luther King Day program sponsored by Alpha Phi Alpha fraternity in Brookhaven on January 15th to address the social justice and human rights initiative. At the February 19th chapter meeting in McComb, Salvation Army Captain Richard Boone presented the chapter with a special award for bell ringing. Hogan coordinated the Student Leadership Conference at Pine Grove Missionary Baptist Church in Summit which was held on September 24th in conjunction with Pine Grove's youth department. Students from school districts in Southwest Mississippi attended the

Conference. Presenters included Pike County Youth Court's Maxine Jones who addressed children of incarcerated parents; District Attorney for Pike, Walthall, and Lincoln counties Dee Bates who addressed cyber bullying; and Phi Mu Omega's own Sheanda Davis who addressed domestic and teen violence. The annual Veterans' Day program at McComb Nursing and Rehab in McComb was co-chaired by Floyd and Jacques. The chapter presented wheelchair bags made of red, white, and blue flag cloth and filled with personal hygiene and entertainment items such as socks, tissue, lotion, puzzle books, etc., and sang patriotic songs to resident veterans. Veterans who attended and spoke were the honorable Percy Robinson and Kenny Cotton, the mayor and police chief respectively of the town of Summit; VFW post commander Melvin Joe Johnson, and a Navy recruiter along with his enlisted wife.

The signature program of the House administration is the Emerging Young Leaders (EYL) program. Phi Mu Omega inducted thirteen girls on July 30, 2011, during a ceremony at the Days Inn in McComb. Inductees were Jazmine Baylor, Kiara Bush, Eyana Montgomery, Alleciah Partman and Sabria Taylor of Denman Junior High School (McComb); Takia Brooks and Tia Bussey of Alexander Junior High School (Brookhaven); TaQuanisha Cotton, Brooklyn Moses, and India Peters of Higgins Middle School (McComb); and Dawson Johnson, Jashia Smith, and Aurianna Vaughn of Wesson Attendance Center (Wesson).

Health-related projects in 2011 consisted of a team for the American Cancer Society's Relay for Life in McComb on May 13 which netted $1135.00 and the breast cancer awareness program. Sheila Sartin suggested a unique project that year—to place symbolic pink ribbon decals on the football helmets worn by players during the entire month of October. Once the chapter had received permission for the project from the Mississippi High School Activities Association, more than 800 players in the McComb, South Pike, Lawrence County, Amite County, North Pike, Lincoln County, and Wilkinson County school districts participated. Commentators made Public Service Announcements during games to acknowledge Phi Mu Omega as the sponsor of the project. The chapter also held a breast cancer awareness program at Bethel AME church in Brookhaven on October 30th. To conclude the health initiatives for 2011, Luckett chaired the annual "Holiday Blood Drive on" December 10th at Wal-Mart in McComb.

The chapter addressed global poverty by providing seeds for African Missionary Janice Robinson, an Amite county native, to take back to a women's group in Kenya. For this purpose, the chapter has continued to supply seeds to Ms. Robinson. A picture of global poverty committee chairman Tammy Witherspoon and member Barbara Scott presenting seeds to the Missionary appeared in the McComb *Enterprise-Journal.*

Due to the ongoing recession dating back to the late 2000's and the continuing fragile recovery into the 2010's, economic security and empowerment issues have continued to be of great concern to the chapter. On February 26, 2011, at the Brookhaven State Bank Community Room, Wilson-McSwain chaired the "Power of a Dream" forum that featured five successful African-American business women. EYL girls attended the forum which Julia Parker moderated. Parker directed questions to panelists author Wanda Jackson of Liberty, MS; Betty Bell of Zeta Delta Omega chapter in Natchez, MS, owner of a consulting firm; Phi Mu Omega members Karen Bryant Luckett, a dentist with a general practice in McComb; "golden girl" Margaret Therrell, co-owner of M & I Tax Services and Southside Carwash in Brookhaven; and Louise Gombako-Amos, an obstetrician-gynecologist and partner in the Women's Health Clinic in McComb. Lanasha Tanner Sanders, also an ob-gyn in the Women's Health Clinic, later reactivated with Phi Mu Omega. The chapter's signature "Jazz by the Lake" at Percy Quin State Park convention center on March 19th furthered this initiative by featuring a live band, a silent and live auction with items donated by local merchants, and foods prepared by several caterers to advertise their businesses. Wilson-McSwain and Luckett co-chaired the event. Scholarships were presented to students at various schools in May (see appendix). Salvation Army bell ringing has continued to be an annual chapter activity. Held on December 3, 2011, at the Lincoln County Multipurpose Building, the Scholarship Ball dinner-dance— the crowning event of each year—featured live entertainment by "4 Real" and culinary treats by Chef's Delight of McComb. That year for Christmas, the chapter allocated funds for a needy family at the request of visionary Jacques, and chapter members made personal contributions to supplement the chapter's donation. The family was grateful for the bicycles and other toys, and the chapter was grateful for the opportunity to end 2011 by being of service to mankind.

Internal leadership training for external service is ongoing. The standards committee presents a list of topics each November for the upcoming year. In addition, members attended statewide clusters and regional conferences during 2010-2013, Boules in 2010 and 2012, Leadership Seminars in 2011 and 2013 and chapter retreats at the Hampton Inn in McComb in 2011 and 2012 and at the Flowering Lotus Meditation and Retreat Center in Magnolia in 2013.

A year and a half into the Stewart administration, Phi Mu Omega elected new officers effective January 2012. Officers were president Marcia Leonard, vice president Ruby Husband, secretary Tammy Witherspoon, assistant secretary Nikki Beckley-Holloway, financial secretary Madeleine Floyd, corresponding secretary Karen Bryant Luckett, treasurer Claudia Moore, hostess Mary Helena Thompson, doorkeeper Doris Jacques, chaplain Sheanda Davis, *Ivy Leaf* reporter Barbara Scott, historian Lorraine Gayden, and parliamentarian Betty Wilson-McSwain. Sheanda Davis replaced Wilson-McSwain as parliamentarian in 2013 (see member roster in appendix). During the presidency of Leonard in 2012 and 2013, the executive committee met monthly in order to implement more efficient and timely chapter meetings. To continue sisterly relations activities that had been initiated by Beckley-Holloway, "First Friday" events included trips to plays at the University of Southern Mississippi in Hattiesburg, bowling, dinner outings, and a fun day at member Valerie Turner's "Sweet Tooth Café'" in downtown Summit. At the "Sweet Tooth", a caricaturist drew and gave each soror her "picture" as a complimentary gift from the Turners.

Leonard prompted committee chairmen to function as expected and even attended and facilitated committee meetings herself when necessary! A "silver star," she epitomizes what an Alpha Kappa Alpha woman should do and be! During her administration, she established short-range and long-term goals, developed a committee reporting schedule, and encouraged the standards committee to continue its Internal Leadership Training (ILT) schedule each year. She also coordinated scholarship ball arrangements in 2012 and 2013 and assisted with the completion of this history.

Chapter activities geared to "Global Leadership Through Timeless Service" in 2012 included the Relay for Life, breast cancer awareness, the holiday blood drive, seed collection and donation, scholarship awards in May, the Veterans' Day program in McComb, Salvation Army bell ringing, and the dinner-dance on December 15th at the National Guard Armory in McComb. Jackson-area band "24/7" provided live entertainment, and Chef's Delight catered the event.

Members Lanasha Tanner-Sanders, Katrina Sartin, Paquita McCray, and Sandra Foxworth reactivated with the chapter in 2013 (see member roster in appendix). In 2013, the chapter attended Martin Luther King Day activities and hosted a refreshment table at a reception following the Alpha Phi Alpha program at Alexander Junior High School on Martin Luther King Day. Beckley-Holloway represented the chapter and facilitated the chapter's participation. The second EYL induction occurred on June 9, 2013, at the Martin Luther King Center in McComb. Inductees were Delicia Bates, Aryielle Carter, Keia Collins, Kimbriona East, Jasmine Harris, Lauren Johns, Essence Lewis, Jasiah Magee, CeUndra McGhee, Abrejha McKennis, Alexandria Nunnery, Callie Sanders, LaDeshia Sims, Xhana Thompson, Chardonay Williiams of Denman Junior High, and Lauren Johnson of North Pike Middle School. The chapter sponsored an EYL "Youth Summit" on July 13th at Higgins Middle School in McComb. Presenters were Delicia Haynes of Xi Mu Omega chapter in Columbia (bullying/cyberbullying) and Phi Mu Omega's Paquita McCray (self-esteem) and Sheanda Davis (teen trafficking). Other presenters were the Town of Summit's police chief Kenny Cotton (domestic violence) and Summit's youngest councilman Daryl Porter (leadership). Terrance Turner, husband of chapter member Valerie Turner, provided the closing motivational remarks. Turner also gave T-shirts and coupons for free ice cream treats from the family-owned "Sweet Tooth Café." The "Youth Summit" concluded with a pizza party for youth, parents, and sorors. Other 2013 projects included planting a community garden at the Summit Academy where Witherspoon is the Adolescent Opportunity Program director, the Veterans' Day program, and the signature Scholarship Ball dinner-dance on December 7th at the Pike County Safe Room in Magnolia.

At the 65th Boule in San Francisco, California, Lorraine Gayden locates her name on the South Eastern region's list of Alpha Kappa Alpha Unforgettable, Unsung Sorors of the Civil Rights Movement.

Emerging Young Leaders (EYL) Youth Summit 2013, pictured left to right, Ayrielle Carter, Lauren Johnson, Callie Sanders, Jasmine Harris, Alexandria Nunnery, LaDeshia Sims, Lauren Johns and Jasiah Magee. Not pictured are: Delicia Bates, Keia Collins, Essence Lewis, Kimbriona East, CeUndra McGhee, Chardonay Williams, Abrejha McKennia and Xhana Thompson.

Phi Mu Omega's 3rd Biannual Cotillion "Simply Elegant". Pictured seated left to right, Ragime Thomas, "Miss Calendar Girl" T'Keyah Jones, Tykesha Faust: back row, Quavondreanna Marshall, Lanessa Jordan, and Xabriella Mallery.

Veterans' Day observance, pictured left to right, Lorraine Gayden, Nancy Denham, Nikkitta Beckley-Holloway, Mayor Percy Robinson, Madeleine Floyd, Betty Wilson-McSwain, Doris Jacques and Mary Helena Thompson.

Chapter X

IN "TIMELESS" SERVICE

Some people just have staying power! This certainly is true of golden, silver, and life members.

Phi Mu Omega is fortunate that it has its share of each of these committed individuals. Currently, the chapter has two active and two former golden girls, eight active silver stars, and five life members.

"Golden" Girls

Nancy W. Denham became the chapter's first fifty-year member at the South Eastern Regional Conference in Memphis, TN, in 2006. An only child, Nancy was born in Chicago, IL. She was initiated into Gamma Phi chapter at Alcorn State University in 1956. She was also a member of Zeta Delta Omega chapter in Natchez. As a charter member of Phi Mu Omega chapter, she has served as financial secretary, hostess, and doorkeeper. She completed further study at Loyola University, Mississippi State University, and Tuskegee University and earned a Master's degree in Education at Mississippi College. She had previously taught in the Natchez, Port Gibson, and Vicksburg school districts, but she retired from the Hazlehurst School District in 1995 after 30 years of dedicated service. She continued in education as a part-time GED instructor at Copiah-Lincoln Community College until she retired in 2012.

Nancy Denham

Doris Jacques

Doris W. Jacques, the visionary organizer of the chapter, and **Margaret W. Therrell** turned golden together at the South Eastern Regional Conference in Nashville, TN, in 2007. Therrell became a general and life member in 2013.

Doris Washington Jacques was born in Summit, Mississippi. She was educated in the McComb, Mississippi, schools and graduated from the all-black Burglund High School in 1954. Doris enrolled at Tuskegee Institute where she received a B.S. degree in Secondary Education. She became a member of Gamma Kappa chapter in 1957. It was at Tuskegee that she met and married her Jamaican husband. Soror Jacques has lived in Canada and Jamaica. In Jamaica, she taught and worked for several Jamaican governmental agencies. When she returned to Summit, she worked for the Southwest Mississippi Mental Health Complex as Coordinator of Records until she retired in December of 1998.

Margaret Wilson Therrell received a B.S. degree from Alcorn State (where she was initiated into Gamma Phi chapter in 1957) and a Master's degree from Tuskegee Institute (now University). She spent 32 years as a chemistry, physics, and biology teacher at the junior high and high school levels. Because of her dedication, she was named Teacher of the Year, Star Teacher, and a Presidential Nominee for Excellence in Science and Math. She also received an Outstanding Teacher's Award. After retirement, she started a second career as an entrepreneur. She is co-owner of the female-owned M & I Tax Services and co-owner of Southside Carwash (both in Brookhaven) with her husband Eugene. A charter member of Phi Mu Omega, Margaret has served the chapter as financial secretary and treasurer. In 2012, she appeared in *Who's Who in Black Mississippi*. Margaret's daughter, Charlotte Therrell Jones, is also a member of Alpha Kappa Alpha. Margaret and her husband have two grandchildren, Nolan and Mackenzie.

Margaret Therrell

Celia Pearson

In 2010, **Celia G. Pearson** became a golden member. Celia became a general and life member in 2011. Celia was born to Emory B. and Ella Cook Gordon in Magnolia, Mississippi. She was influenced to join Alpha Kappa Alpha by her aunt Dr. Dorothy Gordon Gray, a renowned professor at Alcorn, who was instrumental in establishing the first undergraduate chapters in Mississippi. Celia was initiated into Gamma Phi chapter at Alcorn State University in 1960, where she received a B.S. degree in Education. She also holds a Master's degree from California State University, Haywood, CA. She worked as a business teacher in secondary education for 35 years. She retired from the Oakland, CA, school system as an Education Coordinator in 1994 and returned to Mississippi that year.

"Silver" Stars

A few younger chapter members have served Alpha Kappa Alpha from twenty-five to forty-eight years and continue to serve. These members are profiled based on greatest to least time of membership. Thompson and Gayden anxiously anticipate their golden coronations in the next few years! Other chapter "stars" are Hogan, Moore, Scott, Leonard, Luckett, and Wilson-McSwain.

Mary Helena Ross Thompson

Mary Helena Ross Thompson

Mary Helena was born in Columbia, Mississippi. She was initiated into Gamma Phi chapter at Alcorn State University in 1965. She received a B.S. degree in Education from Alcorn and a Master's degree in Elementary Education from Jackson State University. She first taught in the Natchez School District, but she retired from the Franklin County School District in 2002 after 36 years of dedicated service to education. She was instrumental in organizing and securing federally-funded preschools for the Franklin County School District. A charter member of Phi Mu Omega chapter, Mary Helena has served as financial and corresponding secretaries, hostess, and doorkeeper. Her daughter, LaKeisha Thompson Morton of Georgia, is a legacy member of Alpha Kappa Alpha.

Lorraine Gayden

Lorraine Banks Gayden

Lorraine was initiated into Gamma Rho chapter at Jackson State University in 1966. She earned a Bachelor of Arts degree in 1969. She continued her education at Purdue University where she received the Master of Arts degree in English in 1971. Additionally, she earned an Education Specialist degree in secondary education from the University of Southern Mississippi in 1996. Her professional career spanned more than 30 years and included roles as varied as college instructor, community organizer, health planner, quality control supervisor, and Pike County Department of Welfare (now Human Services) Director. She spent her last 14 years before retirement as a high school English teacher at McComb High School. She truly has a heart for service as evidenced by her active involvement in a variety of civic and religious organizations in addition to her dedication to Phi Mu Omega chapter and Alpha Kappa Alpha. She served as charter secretary of Phi Mu Omega. Other positions she has held include vice president, president, *Ivy Leaf* reporter, and historian. In her role as standards committee chairman for many years, she has encouraged fellow chapter members to "Go, Know, and Grow" in knowledge of Alpha Kappa Alpha. This mantra has been demonstrated by her attendance at regional conferences, Boules and Leadership Conferences held by the sorority. As historian, Lorraine accepted the challenge as author of the history of Phi Mu Omega chapter.

Frances Hogan

Frances Bennett Hogan

Frances is a native of McComb. The youngest of 14 children, Frances was one of two of the 14 children in her family to earn a college degree. She holds a B.S. degree in Education from Alcorn State University. While at Alcorn, she became a member of Gamma Phi chapter in 1971. She worked in the private sector for 24 years before changing career paths to enter the teaching profession. At the same time, she furthered her education by earning a M.S. degree in Special Education from Alcorn in 2002 and a M.A. in Supervision and

Administration from the University of Phoenix in 2010. As a charter member of Phi Mu Omega, she has served as president, vice president, secretary, hostess, and custodian. Her daughter Alfonda Renee Westbrook became a legacy member of Phi Mu Omega in 2007.

Claudia Brooks-Moore

Claudia Brooks Moore

Claudia holds a Bachelor and Master of Science in Education from Jackson State University where she graduated Magna Cum Laude. She was initiated into Delta Omicron chapter at Northern Illinois University in 1970. She was a charter member of Xi Nu Omega in Chicago, IL, in 1982. Upon returning to Mississippi in 2006, Claudia joined Phi Mu Omega in 2007 and has served as financial secretary and treasurer. She enjoyed a rewarding career in Federal Civil Service from 1976 to 2004. She held numerous positions with the U.S. Railroad Retirement Board where she was recognized for excellence in service.

Barbara Scott

Barbara Barnes Scott
Barbara was born in Laurel, Mississippi, the daughter of the late Charles and Viola Barnes. She is a graduate of the University of Southern Mississippi where she became a member of Iota Kappa chapter in 1976. Barbara earned Bachelor of Science and Master of Library Science degrees at USM. She was an elementary school teacher and retired as a junior high and high school librarian. Barbara reactivated her membership with the sorority and joined Phi Mu Omega chapter in 2008. She has served as doorkeeper and *Ivy Leaf* reporter. Her most challenging role has been as chairman of the chapter's major fundraiser—the annual Scholarship Ball.

Marcia Leonard

Marcia Scott Leonard
Marcia currently serves as President of Phi Mu Omega chapter. She became a member of Alpha Kappa Alpha at Mississippi Valley State University, Epsilon Pi chapter in 1986. She earned a B.S. degree in Accounting at Grambling State University in Grambling, LA. She has also completed Alternate Route to Education classes at William Carey University in Hattiesburg, MS. She began her career as an accountant at Grambling State. She is presently employed as an accountant at Faust and Associates CPA in McComb. She has served as *Ivy Leaf* reporter, historian, assistant secretary, and vice president. Marcia became a "Silver" Star at the 65th Boule' in San Francisco, CA, in 2012, the same year she became chapter president. A proud year indeed!

Karen Bryant Luckett

Karen Bryant Luckett

Karen was initiated into Gamma Omicron chapter at Tougaloo College in 1986. The following fall, she entered dental school at the University Of Mississippi School Of Dentistry. Unfortunately, the demands of a professional education required a commitment that would not permit her to remain active in the sorority. In 1999, encouraged by her "line sister" Betty Spann, she reactivated her membership and joined the Ivy Omega interest group. This group became Phi Mu Omega chapter which was chartered on January 15, 2000. Betty and Karen served as charter president and vice-president, respectively. During her term, as the second president of Phi Mu Omega, the chapter held its first Membership Intake Process (MIP). Karen has also served as parliamentarian, hostess and corresponding secretary. The year 2011 marked 2 milestones for Karen—Silver Star status and Life membership.

Betty Spann Wilson-McSwain

Betty Spann Wilson-McSwain

Phi Mu Omega chapter began in a dynamic manner under the illustrious leadership of Charter President, Betty Spann Wilson-McSwain. Betty was initiated into Gamma Omicron chapter at Tougaloo College in 1986, where she earned a B.S. degree in Physics. She obtained her Master of Science and Educational Specialist in Educational Leadership at Delta State University and Mississippi College respectively. Betty began her career as a teacher. She has held administrative positions in McComb Public Schools since 1995. She currently serves as Director of Curriculum and Federal Programs. Betty has demonstrated leadership by holding many positions in the chapter and in Alpha Kappa Alpha as well, including serving as Cluster IV Coordinator for the South Eastern Regional Conference in 2002.

"Life" Members

Becoming a life member of the premiere African-American sorority says a lot about commitment to a noble cause and intent to render lifelong service to mankind. Fortunately, Phi Mu Omega has five members who made that all-important commitment and investment.

Claudia Moore
Doris Jacques
Karen Bryant Luckett
Betty Wilson-McSwain
Lorraine B. Gayden

CHAPTER XI

THE BEST IS YET TO COME IN "TIMELESS" SERVICE

The foregoing pages chronicle Phi Mu Omega's inception, programs, projects, and activities, and membership from 1998 through 2013. Optimism remains alive and well—despite any unfavorable economic trends, membership fluctuations, less than enthusiastic involvement of some members, involvement with careers, family obligations, and other concerns that affect the lives of Alpha Kappa Alpha women. Although the chapter is in the early stages of the glorious legacy it expects to create and bequeath to future chapter members, the best is truly yet to come. Among the legacies will be improved chapter efficiency and effectiveness, continued internal membership development and leadership training, constant evaluation and assessment, recruitment and reactivation activities, and an overall increased presence and significance in Southwest Mississippi.

The chapter has established short-range and long-range goals and continues to update and refine these goals following chapter operations surveys each October. Chapter **short-range goals** for operations, programs, and membership are outlined as follows:

Operations
1. Continue monthly executive committee meetings
2. Streamline chapter meeting time utilizing officers and committee chairs according to an established timetable for committee reports and use newer chapter members as co-committee chairs to develop leadership for perpetuity
3. Conduct member development/internal leadership training for all members on a monthly basis using topics selected by the standards committee and approved by the chapter and invite guest trainers as necessitated

4. Train new officers and committee chairs as needed and require additional training at the regional level according to chapter bylaws or the corporate office.
5. Encourage and motivate members to increasingly participate in chapter programs, projects, and activities and
6. Develop more unity through sisterly relations activities "outside" chapter meetings.

Programs
1. Implement significant programs that reflect international initiatives in a timely manner while continuing chapter signature programs
2. Increase the presence and publicity of programs and services and
3. Evaluate programs for impact and significance.

Membership
1. Actively recruit inactive members in chapter's service area.
2. Increase membership by 5% each year through reclamations.

The chapter's **long-range goals** are specified below.

Operations
1. Conduct an MIP every three years or as allowed by corporate office
2. Institute an active mentoring program following an MIP or reactivation and
3. Increase delegate funding in order to facilitate training at the state, regional, and international levels.

Programs
1. Impact 50-100 youth per year for leadership through programs such as EYL, student leadership conferences, teen summits, a calendar girl cotillion, etc.
2. Influence 50-100 youth and adults per year for volunteerism through service projects for cancer awareness, blood drives, Salvation Army bell ringing, a community garden, etc.

3. Increase chapter scholarship awards to $10,000 per year and increase by $1000 annually thereafter in order to provide economic assistance and empowerment to families and youth and

4. Publicize the sorority's Education Advancement Foundation (EAF) scholarship offerings throughout the region at high school and college fairs and through public service announcements or other means.

Membership

Strive for a membership that qualifies as a midsize chapter of 50 members.

Finally, for each chapter member the compilation of this history has poignantly and permanently emphasized the critical need of archiving. This history solidifies the need to control and preserve the inventory of the chapter's historical documents and memorabilia. As laborious as the task was, it taught a valuable lesson to this chapter—and certainly to chapters across the nation and throughout the world—once history is lost, it is lost forever. In the words of historian Earnestine Green McNealey, "Until the lion tells its own story, the story will always glorify the hunter!" Writing this history provided an opportunity for Phi Mu Omega to tell its story from an internal perspective, rather than allowing someone else to tell the story from an external point of view. It is Phi Mu Omega's hope that the sequel chapters to this continuing history will be grander and more glorious. After all, Alpha Kappa Alpha women do "things that are worthwhile."

APPENDICES

Chapter Membership (2000-2013)

Conference/Boule'/Leadership Attendees

Scholarship Recipients

Chapter Awards

CHAPTER MEMBERSHIP
(2000-2013)

Charter Members

2000

Bryant-Patterson, Cynthia
Beckley-Holloway, Nikki
Denham, Nancy
Gayden, Lorraine
Hogan, Frances
Jacques, Doris
Leonard, Marcia
Luckett, Karen
Parker, Julia
Taylor, Zelphia
Therrell, Margaret
Thompson, Mary Helena
Tillman, Esther
Turner, Lillie

2001

Bryant-Patterson, Cynthia
Beckley-Holloway, Nikki
Denham, Nancy
Gayden, Lorraine
Hogan, Frances
Jacques, Doris
Catchings-Jackson, LaTarchia
Leonard, Marcia
Luckett, Karen
Parker, Julia
Pearson, Celia
Taylor, Zelphia

Therrell, Margaret
Thompson, Mary Helena
Tillman, Esther
Turner, Lillie
Watts, Monesa
Young, Yolanda

2002

Beckley-Holloway, Nikki
Denham, Nancy
Gayden, Lorraine
Hogan, Frances
Jacques, Doris
Leonard, Marcia
Luckett, Karen
Parker, Julia
Patterson, Chilibra
Pearson, Celia
Taylor, Zelphia
Therrell, Margaret
Thompson, Mary Helena
Tillman, Esther
Turner, Lillie
Watts, Monesa

2003

Bates, Michelle
Beckley-Holloway
Carr, Tabitha
Dilworth, Velma
Denham, Nancy
Floyd, Madeleine
Gayden, Lorraine
Hogan, Frances
Isaac, Sandra
Jacques, Doris

Leonard, Marcia
Luckett, Karen
Parker, Julia
Shannon, Cora
Therrell, Margaret
Thompson, Mary Helena
Tillman, Esther
Tillman, Joyce
Turner, Lillie
Watts, Monesa
Wilson, Betty
Witherspoon, Tammy

2004

Bates Rolanda, Michelle
Beckley-Holloway, Nikki
Carr, Tabitha
Dilworth, Velma
Denham, Nancy
Floyd, Madeleine
Gayden, Lorraine
Hogan, Frances
Isaac, Sandra
Jacques, Doris
Leonard, Marcia
Luckett, Karen
Parker, Julia
Shannon, Cora
Pearson, Celia
Sharieff, Sharieffah
Therrell, Margaret
Thompson, Mary Helena
Tillman, Esther
Tillman, Joyce
Watts, Monesa
Wilson, Betty
Witherspoon, Tammy

2005

Bates Rolanda, Michelle
Beckley-Holloway, Nikki
Carr, Tabitha
Dilworth, Velma
Denham, Nancy
Floyd, Madeleine
Gayden, Lorraine
Hogan, Frances
Isaac, Sandra
Jacques, Doris
Leonard, Marcia
Luckett, Karen
Parker, Julia
Pearson, Celia
Shannon, Cora
Sharieff, Sharieffah
Therrell, Margaret
Thompson, Mary Helena
Tillman, Esther
Tillman, Joyce
Turner, Valerie
Watts, Monesa
Wilson, Betty
Witherspoon, Tammy

2006

Armistad, Kendra
Bates Rolanda, Michelle
Beckley-Holloway, Nikki
Cockerham, Angela
Carr, Tabitha
Dilworth, Velma
Denham, Nancy
Floyd, Madeleine
Gayden, Lorraine

Hogan, Frances
Houston-Jones, Sheryl
Isaac, Sandra
Jacques, Doris
Leonard, Marcia
Luckett, Karen
Parker, Julia
Pearson, Celia
Shannon, Cora
Sharieff-Bridges, Sharieffah
Therrell, Margaret
Thompson, Mary Helena
Tillman, Esther
Tillman, Joyce
Turner, Valerie
Watts, Monesa
Wilson, Betty
Witherspoon, Tammy

2007

Armistad, Kendra
Bates Rolanda, Michelle
Beckley-Holloway, Nikki
Carr, Tabitha
Cockerham, Angela
Denham, Nancy
Dilworth, Velma
Floyd, Madeleine
Gayden, Lorraine
Hogan, Frances
Houston-Jones, Sheryl
Isaac, Sandra
Jacques, Doris
Leonard, Marcia
Luckett, Karen
Moore, Claudia
Parker, Julia

Pearson, Celia
Shannon, Cora
Sharieff-Bridges, Sharieffah
Therrell, Margaret
Thompson, Mary Helena
Tillman, Esther
Tillman, Joyce
Watts, Monesa
Wilson, Betty
Witherspoon, Tammy

2008

Anderson, Janis
Armistad, Kendra
Carr, Tabitha
Cockerham, Angela
Davis, Sheanda
Denham, Nancy
Dilworth, Velma
Faust, Robin
Floyd, Madeleine
Freeman, Kayla
Gombako-Amos, Louis
Gayden, Lorraine
Hogan, Francis
Holloway, Nikkitta
Husband, Ruby
Isaac, Sandra
Jacques, Doris
Jefferson, Vonnie
Jones, Sheryl
Leonard, Marcia
Lowery, Shirlene
Luckett, Karen
Minor, Marva
Moore, Claudia
Parker, Julia

Pearson, Celia
Powell, Alfonda Renee
Samuels, Janice
Sartin, Sheila
Scott, Barbara
Steptoe, Juanita
Therrell, Margaret
Thomas, Mashanda Lee
Thompson, Mary Helena
Tillman, Esther
Tillman, Joyce
Tillman, Mary Elizabeth
Turner, Valerie
Watts, Monesa
Wilbert, Vanessa
Wilson, Betty
Witherspoon, Tammy

2009

Davis, Sheanda
Denham, Nancy
Faust, Robin
Floyd, Madeleine
Freeman, Kayla
Gombako-Amos, Louise
Gayden, Lorraine
Hogan, Francis
Beckley-Holloway, Nikki
Husband, Ruby
Isaac, Sandra
Jacques, Doris
Jefferson, Vonnie
Leonard, Marcia
Lowery, Shirlene
Luckett, Karen
Wilson-McSwain, Betty
Moore, Claudia

Parker, Julia
Pearson, Celia
Powell, Alfonda Renee
Samuels, Janice
Sartin, Sheila
Scott, Barbara
Steptoe, Juanita
Therrell, Margaret
Thomas, Mashanda
Thompson, Mary Helena
Turner, Valerie
Wilbert, Vanessa
Witherspoon, Tammy

2010

Davis, Sheanda
Denham, Nancy
Faust, Robin
Floyd, Madeleine
Freeman, Kayla
Gombako-Amos, Louise
Gayden, Lorraine
Hogan, Francis
Beckley-Holloway, Nikki
Husband, Ruby
Isaac, Sandra
Jacques, Doris
Jefferson, Vonnie
Leonard, Marcia
Lowery, Shirlene
Luckett, Karen
Moore, Claudia
Parker, Julia
Pearson, Celia
Powell, Alfonda Renee
Samuels, Janice
Sartin, Sheila

Scott, Barbara
Steptoe, Juanita
Therrell, Margaret
Thomas, Mashanda
Thompson, Mary Helena
Turner, Valerie
Wilbert, Vanessa
Wilson-McSwain, Betty
Witherspoon, Tammy

2011

Davis, Sheanda
Denham, Nancy
Faust, Robin
Floyd, Madeleine
Freeman, Kayla
Gombako-Amos, Louise
Gayden, Lorraine
Hogan, Francis
Beckley-Holloway, Nikki
Husband, Ruby
Isaac, Sandra
Jacques, Doris
Leonard, Marcia
Luckett, Karen
Moore, Claudia
Parker, Julia
Samuels, Janice
Sartin, Sheila
Scott, Barbara
Steptoe, Juanita
Therrell, Margaret
Thompson, Mary Helena
Turner, Valerie
Wilson-McSwain, Betty
Witherspoon, Tammy

2012

Beckley-Holloway, Nikki
Davis, Sheanda
Denham, Nancy
Faust, Robin
Floyd, Madeleine
Freeman, Kayla
Gombako-Amos, Louise
Gayden, Lorraine
Husband, Ruby
Isaac, Sandra
Jacques, Doris
Jones, Carol
Leonard, Marcia
Luckett, Karen
Moore, Claudia
Parker, Julia
Sartin, Sheila
Scott, Barbara
Thompson, Mary Helena
Turner, Valerie
Wilson-McSwain, Betty
Witherspoon, Tammy

2013

Beckley-Holloway, Nikki
Davis, Sheanda
Denham, Nancy
Faust, Robin
Floyd, Madeleine
Freeman, Kayla
Gombako-Amos, Louise
Gayden, Lorraine
Hogan, Francis
Husband, Ruby
Isaac, Sandra

Jacques, Doris
Jones, Carol
Leonard, Marcia
Luckett, Karen
McCray, Paquita
Moore, Claudia
Parker, Julia
Pigott-Foxworth, Sandra
Sanders, Lanasha Tanner
Sartin, Katrina
Sartin, Sheila
Scott, Barbara
Thompson, Mary Helena
Turner, Valerie
Wilson-McSwain, Betty
Witherspoon, Tammy

Regional/ Boulé/ Leadership Seminar

Phi Mu Omega South Eastern Regional Conference/Boule/ Leadership Conference Attendance

<u>1999</u>

South Eastern Regional Conference, Montgomery, AL (Ivy Omega Interest Group)
Doris Jacques
Nikkitta Beckley-Holloway
Betty Wilson
Lorraine B. Gayden

Leadership Seminar, Orlando, FL
Betty Spann Wilson

<u>2000</u>
South Eastern Regional Conference, Biloxi, MS (Phi Mu Omega)
Nancy Denham
Lorraine B. Gayden
Doris Jacques
Mary Helena Thompson
Karen Bryant Luckett
Betty Wilson

<u>2001</u>
South Eastern Regional Conference, Tunica, MS
Karen Bryant Luckett

Leadership Seminar, San Juan, Puerto Rico
Karen Bryant Luckett

2002
South Eastern Regional Conference, Huntsville, AL
Karen Bryant Luckett
Celia Pearson
Chilibra Patterson

Boule, Orlando, FL
Betty Wilson

2003
South Eastern Regional Conference, Jackson, MS
Nancy Denham
Lorraine B. Gayden
Frances Hogan
Nikkitta Beckley-Holloway
Margaret Therrell
Julia Parker
Celia Pearson
Betty Spann Wilson

Leadership Seminar, Las Vegas, NV
Lorraine B. Gayden

2004
South Eastern Regional Conference, Nashville, TN
Frances Hogan
Mary Helena Thompson
Betty Spann-Wilson

Boule, Nashville, TN
Lorraine B. Gayden
Frances B. Hogan

2005
South Eastern Regional Conference, Knoxville, TN
Nancy W. Denham
Karen Bryant Luckett

Celia Pearson
Chilibra Patterson

2006
South Eastern Regional Conference, Memphis, TN
Nancy Denham
Velma Dilworth
Madeleine Floyd
Lorraine B. Gayden
Julia Parker
Joyce Tillman
Monesa Watts
Nikkitta Beckley-Holloway

Boule, Detroit, MI
Frances B. Hogan
Lorraine B. Gayden
Madeleine P. Floyd

2007
South Eastern Regional Conference, Nashville, TN
Nikkitta Beckley-Holloway
Tabitha Carr
Sheanda Davis
Lorraine B. Gayden
Frances B. Hogan
Doris Jacques
Marcia S. Leonard
Claudia B. Moore
Margaret Therrell

Leadership Seminar, New Orleans, LA
Nikkitta Beckley-Holloway
Doris Jacques
Betty Wilson
Nancy Denham

Karen Bryant Luckett
Tammy Witherspoon

2008
South Eastern Regional Conference, Montgomery, AL
Lorraine B. Gayden
Frances Hogan
Ruby Husband
Madeleine Floyd
Alfonda Renee Powell
Mary Helena Thompson
Celia Pearson
Tabitha Carr
Shirlene Lowery
Sheila Sartin
Mashanda Thomas
Vanessa Wilbert
Claudia Moore

Centennial Boule, Washington, DC
Nikkitta Beckley-Holloway
Nancy Denham
Karen Bryant Luckett
Lorraine B. Gayden
Frances B. Hogan
Barbara Scott
Claudia Moore
Margaret Therrell
Doris Jacques
Madeleine Floyd
Celia Pearson

2009
South Eastern Regional Conference, Mobile, AL
Madeleine Floyd
Lorraine B. Gayden
Mary Helena Thompson
Frances Hogan

Leadership Seminar, Anchorage, AK
Lorraine B. Gayden

2010
South Eastern Regional Conference, Jackson, MS
Nikkitta Beckley-Holloway
Lorraine B. Gayden
Nancy Denham
Madeleine Floyd
Marcia Leonard
Betty Wilson
Sheanda Davis
Celia Pearson
Vanessa Wilbert
Ruby Husband
Doris Jacques
Karen Bryant Luckett

Boule, St. Louis, MO
Lorraine B. Gayden
Ruby Husband
Doris Jacques
Marcia Leonard
Sheanda Davis

2011
South Eastern Regional Conference, Birmingham, AL
Madeleine Floyd
Lorraine B. Gayden
Ruby Husband
Betty Wilson
Claudia Moore

Leadership Seminar, Atlanta, GA
Madeleine Floyd
Doris Jacques
Marcia Leonard

2012
South Eastern Regional Conference, Chattanooga, TN
Madeleine Floyd
Lorraine B. Gayden
Ruby Husband
Doris Jacques
Marcia Leonard
Tammy Witherspoon

Boule, San Francisco, CA
Marcia Leonard
Barbara Scott
Lorraine B. Gayden

2013
South Eastern Regional Conference, Memphis, TN
Lorraine B. Gayden
Madeleine Floyd
Nancy Denham
Ruby Husband
Robin Faust
Karen Bryant Luckett

Leadership Seminar, Montreal, Quebec, Canada
Lorraine B. Gayden
Ruby Husband

Phi Mu Omega Scholarship Recipients

2001

Stephanie Woodard (MHS) $250
Melissa Hackett (FCHS) $250

2002

Two $250 Scholarships (Names not available)

2003

Two $250 Scholarships (Names not available)

2004

Jessica London $1000
Kayla Brown $1000

2005

Miracle Wilson (Crystal $1000
Springs HS)
Kenesha Cooley $1000
(Hazlehurst HS)

2006

Prenilla White (MHS) $1000 Doris Jacques
Visionary Leadership
Nequanda Harris $1000 Lillie M. Turner Memorial
Adrienne Jones (MHS) $500 Phi Mu Omega
Community Service Award
LaTerrius Lumpkin (MHS) $500 "

Kalethya Walthall (MHS)	$500	"
Tamara Pope (B'haven HS)	$500	"

2007

Arianna Elliot (Crystal Springs HS)	$1000 Lillie M. Turner Memorial
Shambrell Patterson (Amite County HS)	$1000 Doris Jacques Visionary Leadership
(Soror) Valerie McDowell (MHS)	$500 Phi Mu Omega Community Service Award
Destiny Brown (Franklin Co.)	$500 "
Shana Holloway (Hazlehurst HS)	$500 "
Anna Hodges (SPHS)	$500 "

2008

Lynice Higgins	$1000 Doris Jacques Visionary Leadership
Sheronica Chase	$1000 Lillie M. Turner Memorial
Akilah Cotton (MHS)	$500 Phi Mu Omega Community Service Award
KeNeshia Forrest	$500 "
Alisha Rayborn (MHS)	$500 "
Trista Wilson	$500 "
Shameika Woods	$500 "
Akayla Harrell (MHS)	$500 "
April Johnson (MHS)	$500 "

2009

Ebony Patterson (Non-Traditional Student-ABE/GED)	$1000
Cycily Denman (MHS)	$1000 Phi Mu Omega Community Service Award

Sarah Hodges (SPHS)	$1000	"
Paulisha Forrest	$1000	"
Russhele Virgil	$1000	"
Ximena Hawkins	$1500 Doris Jacques	
Kendra Jenkins	$1500 Lillie M. Turner	

2010

Amee Walker (Wilkinson County HS)	$1500 Lillie M. Turner
Jasmine Thompson (SPHS)	$1500 Doris Jacques
Emilia Davis (MHS)	$1000 Phi Mu Omega Community Service Award
Brianna Fuller (Hazlehurst HS)	$1000 "

2011

Cari Hampton (SPHS)	$1500 Lillie M. Turner
Kreshasha Torrence (MHS)	$1500 Doris Jacques
Lisa Powell (SPHS)	$1000 Phi Mu Omega Community Service Award
Taylor Smith	$1000 "
Tessica Wilson (MHS)	$1000 "

2012

Dana Herring (Brookhaven HS)	$1500
Ashley Harris (Lawrence Co. HS)	$1500
Charlis Butler (SPHS)	$1000 Phi Mu Omega Community Service Award
Reagan McNerney (Lawrence Co. HS)	$1000 "

2013

Destiny Pounds (SPHS)	$1500
London Williams (MHS)	$1500
Jimaya Carter (SPHS)	$1000 Phi Mu Omega Community Service Award
Kiplin Taylor (MHS)	$1000 "
Quiara Yarbar	$1000 "

Chapter Awards

2007
Basilei Council Award
Juanita Sims Doty Connections Award
Savannah Jones Black Heritage Award
Diamond NAACP

2008
NAACP Award
Community Health Awareness Award
Basileus Award
EAF Award

2009
NAACP Chapter Membership Award

2010
Portia Trinholm Host Chapter Award

2011
Vanessa Rogers Long Humanitarian Award—Lorraine B. Gayden

Heifer International Award, MS Cluster, Gulf Coast Coliseum, Biloxi, MS, December 2011

2012
Best of the Best "2012" Certificate of Achievement—International Standards Committee

Unforgettable, Unsung Sorors of the Civil Rights Movement—Lorraine B. Gayden—65th Boule, San Francisco, CA

REFERENCES

http://1990'sflashback.com (1990 Economy Prices) George Bush (Accessed 11/25/12)

http://1990's flashback.com (1998 Economy Prices) Bill Clinton (Accessed 11/25/12)

http://1990'sflashback.com/1998/News.asp (Accessed 11/25/12)

http://Clinton3.nara.gov/WH/Work/102899.html—"President Clinton: The Largest Budget Surplus and Debt Pay-Down in History", Oct. 28, 1999 en.Wikipedia.org/wiki/Nelson Mandela (Retrieved 9/15/13)

http://1990'sflashback.com/1997/News.asp(Dolly) Accessed 9/25/12)

www.biography.com/people/Nelson Mandela Retrieved 10/1/13) en.Wikipedia.org/wiki/2000s (decade) (Population and Social issues) (Retrieved 9/13/13)

Ilibagiza, Immaculee (with Steve Erwin) Left to Tell: Discovering God Amidst the Rwandan Holocaust Hay House, Inc. Feb. 15, 2006

Enterprise-Journal, McComb, March 5, 2000, "Carter Co. Closing in Tylertown"

McComb E-J, Jan 19, 2009 "Out of the Darkness", McComb, MS p.1; Tim Woerner en.Wikipedia.org/wiki/Bombing of Iraq (Dec. 1998) accessed 11/23/2012 and 9/24/13

Pike County the Way to Go! Retail Demographics McComb-Pike Co, MS 2010 presented by Pike Co Economic Development District

http://www.gp.com/facility directory/pdf/Mississippi (Georgia Pacific) accessed 9/24/13

www.walthallchamber.com 9/24/13 (creampitcher) Accessed 9/24/13)

www.mccomb-ms.ga/news_detail-T4_RO.php 9/24 (Camellia City) Accessed 9/24/13) en.Wikipedia.org/wiki/Brookhaven-MS (9/24) Accessed 10/1/13)

http://pikeinfo.com(accessed 9/24/13)

www.homeseekersparadise.com (9/24)

http://brookhavenchamber.org/wp (9/24)

www.mccomb_ms.gov/history-of-mccomb_city.php (9/24) en.Wikipedia.org/wiki/McComb-Mississippi 9/24

Enterprise-Journal, McComb, MS, May 28, 2012 "Georgia Pacific"

References

Brookhaven Daily Leader, Jan. 2003

Enterprise-Journal, McComb, MS, April 28, 2005, p.8 "Founders' Day"

http://1990'sflashback.com/1997/News.asp (Accessed 9/25/12)

http://1990'2flashback.com/1998/News.asp (Accessed 9/25/12)

http://en.wikipedia.org/wiki/Timeline_of_United States_history_ (1990%E2%80% 93 present) p. 1-6 Timeline of United States history (1990-present)

http://history1900s.about.com/od/timelines/tp/timeline.htm

History Timeline of the Twentieth Century by Jennifer Rosenberg, About.com Guide

E-J McComb Oct 2004 Breast Cancer Awareness pins Pettway, Jo Celeste History of the South

Eastern Region, 1921-2002

E-J McComb Oct 30, 2007—Proclamation from Mayor for AKA Centennial celebration in 2008

E-J McComb, Nov. 13, 2008, FACES, Oct. 5, 2008, Veterans Day Program, 11/11/05

Carter Co-Walthall (Tylertown plant closing in E-J March 5, 2000) Kellwood Monticello closing Oct. 22, 1999

CNN.com News Net Sept 27, 2000, "President Clinton announces another record budget surplus" White House correspondent Kelly Wallace)

Enterprise-Journal, May 14, 2006 McComb, MS "Mother of the Year"

Ivy Omega Interest Group Packet (June 5, 1999)

Phi Mu Omega Chartering Program (Jan 5, 2000)

Phi Mu Omega Scholarship Ball Souvenir programs/booklets Dec. 2000-2013

Alpha Kappa Alpha Sorority, Inc., Chicago, Illinois, *International Membership Directory* 2009, 100th Anniversary Edition, Harris Connect, LLC

REFERENCES

McNealey, Earnestine Green, *The Pearls of Alpha Kappa Alpha: A History of America's First Black Sorority*, Alpha Kappa Alpha Sorority, Chicago, Illinois, 2010 www.purdue university.edu.in.us. com, email sent March 25, 2013 re Epsilon Rho chapter of AKA

http://web.ics.purdue.edu/ akaep/ (email sent March 25, 2013)
akaep08@yahoo.com (email sent March 25, 2013)

Emerging Young Leaders Membership Program, Phi Mu Omega Chapter, July 30, 2011, Days Inn, McComb, MS
Emerging Young Leaders Membership Program, Phi Mu Omega Chapter, June 9, 2013, Martin Luther King Center, McComb, MS

Emerging Young Leaders Youth Summit, Phi Mu Omega Chapter, July 13, 2013, Higgins Middle School, McComb, MS

Enterprise-Journal, McComb, MS, May 14, 2006, "Mother of the Year"

Alpha Kappa Alpha's Unforgettable, Unsung Sorors of the Civil Rights Movement Exhibit, Moscone Convention Center, San Francisco, CA, July 22-29, 2012

Alpha Kappa Alpha Sorority, Inc., 65th Boule 2012, South Eastern Regional Luncheon, "Sassy in San Francisco: Pink Pearls or Pink Pumps or Pink Purses" program, July 26, 2012, San Francisco Marriott Marquis (Salon 8)

Education Week, ESEA of 1965, August 4, 2004, (updated Sept. 19, 2011)
Education Week, NCLB Act Reauthorized by George Bush in 2001
Minutes, Phi Mu Omega, January-May; August-October 2013
Phi Mu Omega Handbook 2001
Phi Mu Omega Scholarship Ball Souvenir programs

REFERENCES

Phi Mu Omega Chapter Scrapbook (2000-2013)

Phi Mu Chartering Program, January 15, 2000

Ivy Omega Interest Group Packet (June 5, 1999)

Phi Mu Omega chapter narrative histories

Enterprise-*Journal,* McComb, MS, March 19, 2005, "Founders' Day"

The Spirit Within: Voices of Young Authors, Vol. I, Metropolitan Teaching and Learning Center, Chicago, IL, January 2004, Jason Powe, Judy Rosenbaum, Diane

The Spirit Within: Voices of Young Authors, Vol. II, 2006, Alpha Kappa Alpha Sorority, Inc., Chicago, IL, Creative Curriculum Initiatives

References

Chicago Tribune, March 9, 2010, Obituary of Linda Marie White

Ivy Leaf, Fall 2007, "Jazz on the Lake", p. 85

Brookhaven Daily Leader, January 9, 2011, "2010 State Cluster in Greenville"

Brookhaven Daily Leader, Oct. 23, 2011, "Student Leadership Conference"

Enterprise-Journal, McComb, MS, Nov. 2011, "Student Leadership Conference"

Woodville Republican, Nov. 24, 2011, "Veterans' Day Program in Centreville"

Hometown: A Remembrance, Mac Gordon, Magnolia Gazette Publishing Corporation, Magnolia, Mississippi 2011

INDEX